Japan: Doing Business in a Unique Culture

Published by **Boson Books,** an imprint of C & M Online Media, Inc.

Raleigh, North Carolina

bosonbooks.com

Design by Once Removed

ISBN 1-932-48232-6

Japan: Doing Business in a Unique Culture

Kevin Bucknall

Raleigh, NC

Contents

Tables

Preface

This book is about good manners and was written with business people and public servants in mind, but some of the advice will also be useful to those visiting Japan as tourists. In recent years, advances in technology have speeded up transport and communications and some might think that this makes dealing with foreigners easier. In fact the opposite can be true: we now have so much more opportunity to accidentally insult those from a different nation. What is considered to be proper manners that work well for you in your society might not do so in a different one and could even create problems. If you want to succeed, perhaps sell technology, buy products at the best price, or sign an agreement between your government and theirs, then you might have to make changes in your normal approach, behavior or dress style.

When visiting Japan, you will get on better if you act in ways that they consider to be polite. Behavior and style are extremely important to the Japanese and they spend much of their lives making sure that they do things properly. In our culture we often do things in any way that seems convenient at the time but in Japan many actions have to be done in a closely prescribed way. An observant outsider might notice and remember the way their Japanese counterparts do a few things and in this way learn about the behavior considered "proper", but the same observer is unlikely to notice all. And more to the point, however observant we are, we almost never notice the things they avoid doing. This book will help you learn both what to do and things to shun.

If you are there on business it is particularly important to behave in an acceptable manner, because this can speed up the all-important development of your relationship and shorten your stay. This saves you both time and money. Behavior seen as proper is also likely to improve your chance of actually reaching agreement, so it is really worth making the effort.

You should not think that "doing things their way" is in any way dishonorable or demeaning. You might find yourself wondering "Why must I do it their way, why don't they do it mine", but remember that you want to sell, buy, sign or whatever, and a few sympathetic changes in your behavior can help you gain what you want. This said, you might feel that some suggestions are unacceptable, for instance on the grounds of political correctness. Fine! At least you are making a choice and you know what is involved.

Chapters 1 and 2 provide information about the main elements of Japanese culture and offer some general advice on how to behave. Chapter 3 considers what you should do in your first approach to the country and in Chapter 4 you get help with the tricky business of choosing your team. Chapter Five 5 deals with the early meetings, and Chapter 6 goes on to cover the later ones, providing suggestions for improving your negotiating skills. Chapter 7 looks at common Japanese tactics. The important issue of socializing is covered in Chapter 8, while Chapter 9 provides help and advice on what to expect if you go to live and work in Japan. Chapter 10 covers how to treat a Japanese team visiting your country. Finally, In Chapter 11 there is special advice to the women readers of this book. If you are male but likely to have a female on your team, this chapter should also be considered required reading.

You might notice an occasional repetition of advice in different chapters; this is deliberate, as some particular point made earlier might be particularly important in a new context and I felt a reminder would do no harm.

You will be aware that societies are always in a process of change, so that the advice given here covers the tried and tested ways. The younger generation is starting to change, sometimes quite radically, and before too long some of the advice offered here will doubtless seem a little old-fashioned. However, research tends to show that although Asian youngsters readily adopt the consumerist trappings of Western society, they often cling to their own traditional values, reverting to them as they grow older. More importantly, youngsters in Japan are rarely given real power so that the important people you deal with tend to be more advanced in years. The advice is aimed squarely at dealing with the older power holders, which is where a favorable (to you) decision can be made.

You should bear in mind a few things. First, with this kind of advice there is a danger of stereotyping and thinking that each person you meet must fit the typical mould. Remember that not everyone is identical and that you will probably encounter individuals who do not seem to fit too well. This may be because some are ignorant of the niceties of accepted good manners, owing to factors like class background, family dysfunction, or a different geographical location; others are aware of how to behave but simply do not care much.

Second, when doing business it helps immensely if you know about the culture and appropriate ways of negotiating as it can give you a strong edge over your competitors. Yet it must be seen as a valuable extra tool not a substitute for your other management skills. You still need the normal good business practices of being mentally agile, creative, able to negotiate well, make good decisions, and stitch together favorable deals.

Third, do not be put off by the amount there seems to be to learn – even a little bit helps, and each time you negotiate or socialize with Japanese business people or officials you will notice things and find yourself understanding and remembering more. You do not have to slavishly follow all the advice and it is possible, for example, for foreign, young, bearded, extrovert males (not ideally suited to succeed in Japan) to do well – but it is harder for them and tends to take them longer before their efforts are crowned with success.

Fourth, reading and learning in advance should reduce the degree of culture shock that you will probably experience the first few times you visit Japan. This will help you by reducing the tiredness caused by a battering of unexpected and what might seem strange behavior and procedures. With more energy you can expect to operate more effectively.

Adopting political correctness of the Western kind can be tricky in Japan, where male superiority is not questioned by the majority. Mostly you will be dealing with male power holders; the women you encounter will probably be young and attractive "Office Ladies" (OL's), rather than people of authority. I have largely stuck to using "he" throughout the book to reflect this situation.

Disclaimer: the advice in this book is offered without prejudice and the author cannot be held responsible for any losses you might incur. In return, he does not expect to share in any profits that you might make!

Introduction

Japan still clings to many feudal values

The nation is closer to feudal values than most developed countries. It has begun the process of moving towards values more appropriate to a modern nation but there is still a way to go.

One feudal value is that women are granted low status in the masculine-dominated society. Even here there has been some change – over half of all women now go out to work and some women are successfully carving out career paths.

A second example of the persistence of old values is the principle of a job for life, at least in the large companies with famous names. Until recently, in a major Japanese company, the relationship between the worker and his company was close and involved mutual loyalties, not unlike that of a marriage. Dismissing workers, like divorce, is still felt to be an extremely serious event. However, this began to weaken in the 1990s and it is increasingly possible to dismiss surplus workers. If doing business in Japan you are likely to be dealing with just such a major company; but behind this front rank there has always been a mass of many small firms, which give few perks, pay their employees less, and get rid of them when they are not needed. Slowly, the major companies are starting to follow suit.

Another ancient value is that the old are venerated and youth waits its turn. Promotion is still largely by age not merit (although this too is beginning to change) and most people with power are relatively old.

A fourth rather feudal view is the Japanese preference for Mercantilism, which involves a protectionist view of the economy, so that it is felt desirable to keep imports low, exports high, and accumulate foreign exchange. This policy proved to be successful in the past and, despite a growing realization that it now limits progress, it still seems to be supported by the majority.

Another feudal view is that the rule of law is not particularly important. Established business relationships and friendships are more central and are heavily relied upon. Change has started here, and increasingly people are beginning to recognize the benefit of contracts and the rule of law but personal relationships remain crucial to most Japanese.

A sixth traditional view concerns cooperation and the group. Group feeling is powerful; loyalty to it is strong and individualism has always taken a back seat. Competition between individuals is rare but competition between groups is normal. Change has begun and the concept of the group is weakening slightly - the young are a bit more individualistic than in the past.

In Japan the public service dominates private industry, and together they make up a less than fully competitive system. Despite being a democratic country, in many ways the public service is stronger than the elected government and determines much domestic policy. In the mid 1990s, the bureaucracy began to lose a little of its previously dominant role. It was demonstrated that the Ministry of Finance had mismanaged housing-loan companies which had over-lent to speculators, while the Health Ministry had succeeded in allowing blood contaminated with AIDS to be distributed. As a result of these and other incidents, people are beginning to look on bureaucrats with more critical eyes. The power of monopoly groups is also under attack; in 1996, the domestic monopoly in telecommunications held by the Nippon Telegraph and Telephone Corporation (NTT) was ended and in 2005 Japan's lower house of parliament passed Prime Minister Junichiro Koizumi's plan to privatize the post office .

Recent Changes

Prior to 1990 Japan was often seen as the major success story among developed nations and one from which many useful lessons could be learned. Innumerable books appeared describing and explaining "the Japanese miracle" so that Western nations could improve their performance. It has been some years since this event last occurred.

The "bubble economy" of the 1980s burst and, starting in 1991, Japan entered a recession which so far has not ended, although early signs that it might be near the end began to appear in 2003-4 but without going anywhere much.

Japan is altering, albeit slowly. The long drawn out recession was the trigger for change, but behind it lays the fact that the Japan is now a mature economy and the old feudal approaches and systems that worked so well in the past are no longer appropriate. As long as things were going well, this fact could be concealed, but when the system was eventually placed under pressure, the weaknesses become evident.

Another cause of change has been steady pressure from abroad, led by the United States, for Japan to open up its economy to greater foreign access and to reduce or remove the many barriers to imports. If and when Japan moves to deregulate the protected and bureaucrat-dominated economy, we can expect satisfactory economic growth to resume. This pressure has slackened under President George W. Bush, as America itself began to be more concerned with direct protection of domestic interests and less in favor of promoting global competition.

A further pressure for change has been the penalty of success. In the past, Japan's rapid growth and successful export penetration of world markets caused the yen to appreciate. The high valued yen and an expectation of steadily increasing wages over life resulted in higher production costs which eventually led to a migration of manufacturing industry abroad. This largely went to the more rapidly growing Asian countries, but some moved to Europe and North America. This is popularly known in Japan as the "hollowing out" of the economy. The share of manufacturing industry in real Gross Domestic Product started to decline in 1992.

It is worth noting that despite the recession, the people still enjoy the second highest standard of living in the world – as they did before it began! This is indeed a very rich country.

The recession has had its effect and the country is going through a period of economic change. After decades as a leading industrial country selling highly desirable consumer durables on international markets, Japan is in the process of re-establishing itself as a service nation. By 1980 Japanese concern about the hollowing out of the economy was clear. The process worries many Japanese but is in fact merely the result of rapid economic development and growing wealth that has caused wages to increase, so rendering manufacturing increasingly uncompetitive. Hollowing out is the price of success.

The economic change induced or accelerated by recession is already starting to affect social values and attitudes in this highly conservative nation. The Japanese way of doing things has started to change.

Unemployment is regarded as shameful in Japan, so many white-collar workers who have been declared redundant hide this fact from their families and dutifully dress and go off to work each morning but spend it in parks and other places, rather than admit the truth. The suicide rate hit new peaks in the early years of the 21st Century, probably as a result of this.

Deflation has been a problem since the late 1990s and it has prevented some domestic investment from taking place; it is easy to make something and sell it on at a paper profit when prices are rising, but with deflation, an apparent loss is off-putting. Many households have large savings and they have benefited from falling retail prices, as the real value of the savings has increased. Pensioners do reasonably well from deflation of course, and the population is ageing rapidly, so that consumption is kept up.

Following the bursting of the economic bubble, house prices collapsed (some residences fell to about a quarter of their previous value) and repayments cannot always be kept up. Homeless people have appeared in the major cities.

Crime, low by international standards, is on the increase and events like the 1995 sarin gas attack in a Tokyo subway shock and worry people. The traditional gangsters of Japan, the yakuza, are easily identified by their tight curly-hair perms, lavish lurid tattoos and often a missing finger. Once regarded as folk-heroes almost like modern day samurai, they have been under government pressure since the early 1990s and many are now in effect redundant. It is difficult for them to find new work, especially given the shortage of fingers which allows them to be easily identified. The market has developed an interesting solution: at least one doctor specializes in fitting prosthetic fingers to ex-yakuza would-be job applicants! Related to this issue, the cartoons of Mickey Mouse and Minnie, both of whom lack a digit, remind some people of yakuza.

Scandals involving the financial sector, including grossly inefficient banks many of which carry huge bad debts and overvalued shares as "assets", are a prime cause of concern to many and so far there have been few reforms.

Many urban youth are reconsidering the traditional values of their elders, but even the elderly are starting to want something better than the events that they see around them. The old sense of belonging to a secure and worthwhile group, known as "Japanese", is being eroded.

One: The Most Important Elements in the Culture

Self-Awareness, the Group, and Conformity

The Japanese are one of the most homogenous nations in the world
Japan has been isolated by both geography and choice for many centuries so that relatively few foreigners live there. Marrying a foreigner has always been virtually taboo and, although it has started to become a bit more respectable, it is still not encouraged. Some 98.5 per cent of the residents of Japan are ethnic Japanese and the remainder are mostly Koreans, who often look Japanese to the casual eye. Koreans are one of only two sizeable minority groups resident in Japan, the other being Chinese.

Japan possesses a long and rich cultural history although many of the basic elements originated abroad, especially in China. Almost all Japanese are strongly aware and proud of their nationality. There is a deep fascination with the culture, history, and society and it would seem that for many, the proper study of mankind is Japan. The uniqueness is taken for granted and is a strong source of satisfaction. There is a major degree of self-absorption and a widespread interest in questions like "What does being Japanese mean?", "Why has Japan been so economically successful?" and "What should be the role of Japan in the world?"

Despite the general homogeneity, there are some minor regional differences; in particular the Eastern areas facing the Pacific Ocean are seen as more outward looking when compared with the parts facing the Sea of Japan. Another important difference exists between Kansai (the old traditional area that includes Kyoto and Osaka) and Kanto, the Tokyo area, which represents modern Japan - accents, art, and cooking styles all differ.

The consciousness of being Japanese is part of a strong nationalism
These deep feelings of nationalism are tapped by Japanese firms which for years successfully sold the idea that imports are generally inferior, are not suited to local habits or lifestyles, or might even be dangerous to health. For instance, many Japanese believe that they cannot eat imported rice without suffering indigestion. Similarly, consumers often used to prefer to buy Japanese products, even if they

1

were more expensive. This was one of several reasons why foreign firms found it difficult to penetrate the Japanese market.

The recession that began in 1991 brought unemployment and as belts tightened people began to seek cheaper products even if they were imported. This has allowed foreign firms more access and American cash-and-carry stores have opened. Foreign beef is now actually sought, especially since the arrival of BSE in Japan in 2001. Old habits die hard but the old "buy the best at any price" attitudes have begun to wane. This can be seen in magazines aimed at consumers – once they focused on the best; now they run articles on where to buy cheaply.

The desire to conform is strongly built into the national psyche

It is widely held that it is dangerous for an individual to distance himself or herself from the group: one should do what the others are doing and not buck the trend. There is a well-known folk-saying that it is the nail that stands up that always gets hammered down. You might remember that it is a mistake to try to get a Japanese to act in a way that would make him or her stand out from the crowd. They will often not be able to comply, and if they try to do so, they will feel awkward and resent you for it.

Table 1.1 The strong urge to conform can be seen in things such as

The uniform-like sameness of clothing that is essential in the business world
The identical apparel necessary in virtually all sports or leisure activities
The sudden sweeping crazes for a single leisure activity
The standardized lunch boxes and back packs which schoolchildren carry
The identical raincoats worn by children and young students

Harmony in group relations is heavily prized

People go to great lengths to avoid any action that would disrupt the harmony of the group (*wa*). The effort to keep harmony increases the level of hidden stress and there are usually strong undercurrents and rumors circulating behind the scenes. Perhaps to help defuse the stress of having to constantly behave correctly, Japanese adult males often enjoy reading thick *manga* comics, some of which feature a hero totally unconstrained by any social mores and contain sex, sadism and violence. You might notice men openly reading them on trains or subways; there is no stigma attached to this. Some Japanese television programmes also involve extreme violence or are grossly humiliating to the individual concerned, and probably serve a similar function of cathartic release.

Group harmony is everywhere and can be broken in unusual ways, for example, when on a train some Japanese prefer not to have a foreigner join their coach as they feel that it upsets the peaceful harmony of the existing group. There is a vague fear, although not articulated, that foreigners could do something unexpected and this worries people. They will, however, still be polite to you.

There is no strong class system in Japan

Japan moved so rapidly from a feudal society with a strong rural basis to a modern urban industrial society that it avoided the build up of a large working class with an awareness of its identity and bound by feelings of antagonism towards the ruling classes in theoretical Marxist fashion. Consequently, there are few feelings of the "us and them" kind. Despite this, the descendants of the samurai class and old rich families are definitely better placed to get their children into the top educational establishments and from there into positions of authority. It is hierarchy without modern class warfare.

Young Japanese sent abroad to study

Quite often young Japanese are sent to English-speaking countries like America or England to study. In Japan they are subject to rigid expectations about their behavior and need to conform; in contrast, while abroad they may engage in extreme forms of dress or dye their hair blond etc. This is particularly likely if a small group bands together. Each person knows that this is their main chance to be different and express rebellious attitudes. If you have encountered punk or otherwise extreme individuals in your country, be aware that this may not be the norm when they return to Japan. Should you come across one later, working in Japan and dressed very formally, it would be extremely unwise to mention the brief period of rebellion, especially in front of other Japanese.

This said, some youngsters in large Japanese cities are starting to dress and behave in ways considered both extreme and offensive by their elders. In major cities you can expect to see youth with colored hair or curly hair, and wearing lurid clothing, often mixed in somewhat surprising ways. A generation gap has appeared and is gradually widening (see below, p.4-6).

Social Changes

Outside influences are strong

The Japanese people usually regard their culture as unique, but it is surprisingly eclectic and open to outside influences. The written language came from China and the Buddhist religion from Korea. The Japanese language itself is full of English words which are generally liked and used widely. This contrasts strongly with France, where borrowing foreign words is officially frowned upon and resisted by the state. In Japan, foreign sports and fashions are avidly seized upon and modern technology has been quickly accepted, often improved, and then disseminated widely. If this issue arises in conversation, it would be a good idea for you to praise the flexible way they have used and often improved upon the import.

The Second World War is a touchy subject

In Japan, this is called "The Pacific War". The dropping of the atom bomb, as well as the ultimate defeat, had a major impact on people. The culture has a strong central core which sees things as either being right and proper or else totally wrong; to lose is improper and hence is unacceptable. In addition the Japanese perceive themselves as being generally superior: for an individual to lose at anything is regarded as a disgrace but to lose to a foreigner is an even greater blow to self-esteem. The occupation by the United States immediately after the war was traumatic and struck a severe blow to the accepted image of themselves. It not only underlined the failure, it also brought in by force various Western (mainly North American) liberal institutions and a new Constitution which many resented.

As can be imagined, the behavior of some of the foreign troops was alien and often offensive. As a result, some older Japanese have something of a love-hate relationship with the United States. Note that should the Pacific War or post war period be raised with you (you should never do so), it is customary to refer to the occupying powers as "The American visitors", and you should avoid the words "Occupation" and "Occupiers" as they would not endear you.

The generation gap

A generation gap has begun to open up as younger Japanese start to go their own way, although there is still widespread veneration of the elderly. The older generation is often aware of Japanese atrocities committed in China and South East Asia but ignore and try to repress the memory. In contrast, most of the youth have been deliberately kept in ignorance by the centralized and conformist educational system, which glosses over any reprehensible behavior and presents Japan as a simple victim of the war. The youth are told repeatedly about the atom bombing of Japan, which is well publicized in an annual commemoration of the bombing of Hiroshima on August 6th 1945. The refusal to depict Japan as anything other than a victim in World War Two began to fray at the edges in the 1990s but still persists.

What are the youngsters coming to?

A popular topic of conversation among Japanese adults is the behavior of young people, particularly their questioning of traditional values such as group loyalty and conformity. A small but increasing number of younger Japanese are beginning to act independently and eschew the group. It is possible to meet single Japanese males cycling around countries like Australia, rather than going abroad in groups on organized tours. Even the identification of self with work has weakened a little and a few males are spending more time at home with the wife and children, and will even take more of their holiday entitlement to do this.

Many older people worry about such changes in youth and the challenge to traditional values. Some of the elderly condemn the new generation in bitter terms, believing that they are rejecting an essential part of what is seen as "Being Japanese". It disturbs them, for example, that the young no longer bow formally on the street when encountering someone they know, and they worry that selfish individualism seems to be on the increase. This is frequently felt to be a disease imported from the West.

The increasing numbers of Japanese studying abroad may eventually increase the pace of change, including the adoption of new ideas and a more creative approach in business, but so far the young tend to be frustrated by the system and are often eventually forced back into more traditional modes of behavior if they wish to advance their careers.

One significant feature is that a small number of intelligent, well-educated youngsters are no longer following the traditional path of joining a top company and working their way up. Instead, they are choosing to set up their own businesses, particularly in the arts and creative areas. Such people are often the more successful youngsters or at least those who are trying hard. Behind them are unknown numbers of disenchanted youth, unemployed and living off their parents or moving from low-paid job to job. They appear to live to party. With an emphasis on way-out clothing, music and, until magic mushrooms were recently made illegal, psychedelic drug trips, it is very reminiscent of Swinging London in the 1960s or Haight-Ashbury around 1967. It is too soon to know if this trend of disenchanted youth will continue or merely be another short-lived fad.

Art and Culture

Symbolism matters much

Symbolism goes back a long way and people are constantly on the lookout for it. They will examine the actual words used in conversations and any gestures that may accompany the chosen phrase. It is not only what is said and done that is considered, for people watch for things that are not being done or said and ask themselves why.

It is useful to remember a few of the symbols in Table 1.2 (below) because you will come across them and can then make an appropriate comment. Symbolism is often a good topic of conversation if you are stuck. A comment by you about the painting on the wall of the meeting room, for example, might allow you to gain credibility and assist you in your negotiations. It shows that you have done your homework well, without you having to say anything that could be considered boastful or arrogant. More than that, it demonstrates an interest in Japan which most Japanese find hard to resist.

In the West, an awareness of seasons and their changes, once so much a part of rural and peasant life that it was taken for granted, has largely disappeared. By contrast, in Japan there is still a strong identification with the periodic flow through the year. Each season brings its own relevant symbol, often drawn from agriculture. For example, such things as the first plum, the first tea, and the first rice are important to many people. They will take pride in buying them and serving them to family and friends, who will be expected to recognize the event as a sort of minor milestone marking the passing of time. As part of a seasonal awareness, most Japanese do not normally swim after August and it might be better if you did not suggest going for a dip after that.

Nature is beautiful – but only when tamed

Beauty and nature have a strong place in Japanese traditional culture. As a component of their view of life and the world, the Japanese feel a sort of "ongoingness" in both nature and life, of which they are a part. The Shinto religion with its stress on nature as central and the relatively unimportance of humans when set in the natural landscape is influential here. However, nature in the raw is considered to be only the crude essence and it is essentially too inelegant; man is also a part of nature and should mould it to an even greater perfection.

Table 1.2 Some standard symbolism in the arts

Pine tree	Long life
Bamboo	Constancy and virtue
Fern	Expanding good fortune
Lobster	Old age
Carp fish	Strength and determination (good for boys)
Peach blossom	Happiness in marriage and the feminine virtues of softness, mildness and peacefulness (good for girls)
Sweet potato	Struggle of the poor to survive
Pine needles	Marital fidelity
Mandarin ducks	Marital fidelity

This strong feeling for nature, accompanied by a need to shape it, can be seen in the composition of Japanese paintings; in the way flowers are arranged; or the design and placement of rocks, lakes and temples in parks and gardens. This "take and improve" approach is also evident in the treatment of imported technology.

The memory can beat the actual event

An important part of culture and art was the *recollection* of a scene or event. This might have been regarded as inspiring at the time, but the memory of the event would often be seen as even more important and make up something truly beautiful. In the past, the recollection could be assisted by the person writing a poem to commemorate and record the main milestones in his or her life. These might include such things as visits to another place, family gatherings, marriages, or the arrival of the first born child.

A poem might also be composed as a result of feelings created by something beautiful in nature, such as falling autumn leaves or seeing a mountain spring at dawn. When read years later, the true spiritual beauty of the event is reinforced and solidified, developing a new and deeper meaning.

The widespread taking of photographs by Japanese travelling abroad seems to be the contemporary version of writing a poem and may serve a similar need.

Work and Hierarchy

Only the best is good enough

Do note that the Japanese strive for total professionalism in whatever they do. Any task is taken seriously, and is normally done with careful dedication. Employees at all levels are expected to seek perfection and most try to do so. This is true even of low grade workers, who often wear a simple uniform, such as a headband, to show they are a dedicated, hardworking and supportive member of the group. The general attitude is that there is only one way of doing a job properly and it will be followed. Zen Buddhism encourages this view, seeing the world in terms of either right or wrong. A person should not be wishy-washy and fudge things, but do things properly. If as a foreigner you do something the right way they might see it - but if you do it the wrong way you can guarantee that they will notice at once.

The high quality achieved in products such as motorcars, cameras, and TV sets is a manifestation of this dedicated approach. Taking extreme care with details shows in Japanese flower arranging, Japanese gardens, the pretty way that food is arranged on plates, and the sudden group crazes for an introduced Western sport or commodity but which require particular dress or way of using it. The famous Japanese tea ceremony is an example, where the room itself, the simple decoration, the utensils used and even the movements made are precisely defined and must be followed. In Japan, training and education are highly valued, as befits the quest for professionalism and perfection. Training and retraining of workers is a constant feature of many Japanese firms.

Hard work is regarded as normal

Companies expect their workers to voluntarily give up their evenings or part of the weekend to work or engage in work-related social activities. Hardly any staff members seem to take all of their allotted annual holidays. Lunch times are commonly restricted to half-an-hour and few people will drink alcohol in the middle of the day as it might impair performance. Excluding Australia and New Zealand, in

2003, the Japanese worked longer hours than any other developed nation. Attitudes are weakening over time, for in 1979 the average employed person worked 2,126 hours a year (USA 1,833) but only 1,801 hours in 2003 (USA 1,792) A preference for more leisure time has appeared and Japan is starting to resemble other developed countries. However, differences in recording methods probably underestimate the hours actually worked in Japan which in turn overestimates the convergence.

Gender Roles

Like Thursday's Child, Women's Lib. still has far to go
Japan is not a country where Women's Lib. has made much inroad. Although the Constitution guarantees equality, this does not in fact exist. Japanese males do not regard women as equals and most would subscribe to the view that "A woman's place is in the home". Note that few Japanese males would be interested in hearing about the feminist movement in your country! In Japanese companies, most women are young and engaged in mundane low-level jobs like typing and filing. A demure attitude is demanded of women, and their eyes are generally kept downcast in the presence of men. Few women will voice an opinion even in the unlikely event of being asked.

The Office Ladies or "Fragrant Flowers"
Young Japanese women in white-collar work are generally known as "Office Ladies" and referred to as "OLs". Their main function is to be young, decorative, well dressed, and fragrant, in order to brighten up the men's workday. In the evening they are expected to engage in mindless and frivolous entertainment. While at work they are only entrusted with minor tasks like making tea for the men and doing the photocopying. They are often expected to get in early to do mundane chores like dusting and cleaning. It is assumed that women will marry and leave work by their mid-twenties, after which they are disparagingly referred to as "Christmas cakes" (She's no good after the 25th!) In many companies a woman must resign if she marries.
It is difficult for the intelligent and earnest-minded professional woman to be taken seriously; many of them have to serve a lengthy period of time undertaking mindless repetitive tasks before they can start to rise in their career path.
In the business world, male networks are extensive and bonding activities are commonplace, normally being held after work hours or at

the weekend. They include attending various sporting activities and going out for an evening's eating and drinking. Women have no place here: this is a hidden but powerful brake on their advancement.

The role of men

Men are expected to be married by 35 years of age, i.e., about ten years older than for women. The function of the male is to earn sufficient money to take care of his family, which involves working hard, spending long hours at the company, and gaining promotion. There is little feeling that he should be at home, share in family life, help raise the children, or even love his wife, although he is expected to sire children. Once that has been achieved, he is largely perceived as a mere breadwinner and status-earner for the family. In general, the Japanese males are not really comfortable with modern Western views about the position and progress of women, nor the career-mindedness of modern Western women. To many it seems both alien and threatening.

The power of the wife

In Japan, the power of women is still largely restricted to the home, where they play a major role. They are expected to bear children, and are then responsible for bringing them up, virtually alone. They tend to spoil their children, especially the boys, and make the decisions about their education (although the husband would be consulted). A common term for a wife is *okusan*, which exactly translates as "Her Indoors", the same term used by Arthur Daley in the British TV show *Minder*. One of her steady tasks is to do the shopping, as most Japanese prefer fresh food bought daily and the tiny urban apartments allow little space for food storage in any case. Some change in these views is occurring in the new millennium and corner stores are beginning to reduce in number.

The wife maintains a tight control over the purse strings: the husband hands over his monthly salary and the wife then gives her husband his daily spending money. This is often presented as indicating that she has real power in the family, but to my mind it really reflects weakness: the husband is never there and so is not able to make decisions about household expenditures. When the wife takes over this responsibility, it allows him to spend even more time away from home, drinking with colleagues and friends and carousing in bars and restaurants. Wifely control over the finances does actually prevent him from spending all his salary outside the house which would result in the family suffering.

There is growing dissatisfaction among young women about their status and role, but only a little real change. A few highly competent women have succeeded in politics and business, but they have to be a lot better than the men at their level to do so.

The attitude towards women is definitely changing – a bit

Such attitudes towards women are still the most common, although there has been some relaxation and changes since the 1980s. A shortage of skilled labour is slowly eroding the traditional view that women have to resign on marriage and especially if they have a child, and a small, but growing, number of women are developing a career path. Younger Japanese in particular are changing their attitudes and becoming less "Japanese" in their views about the proper roles of husband and wife but they can still find it difficult to alter things. Over half of Japanese women are in the work force, but in the main they still occupy the lower positions.

The recent recession has meant less overtime at work and more time for some husbands to get home early enough to see their children before bed and participate at least a little in household chores. Older married men are still not generally expected to help around the house, cook, clean or shop. With younger couples, husbands are starting to do a bit along these lines, particularly if no outsider can actually see them doing it. The Japanese are not in agreement on whether this is a real and permanent change. Some observers express doubt that the young husbands will persist in helping around the house: they think that when the recession ends the men folk will revert to type and stay late at work or go out drinking with their colleagues. Others feel that it is more likely that they will revert to type after a few years as they grow older in any case. Few married men will take their wives out in the evening for pleasure, and those who do are virtually all young.

A surprising change occurred back in 1993, when it suddenly became the fashion for young unmarried women to dress in wild brief costumes that possessed more than overtones of bondage and S & M, and to attend rave clubs after work. This contrasts sharply with traditional demands on women and their demure and silent behavior while at work. It seems to be part of a changing and increasingly rebellious attitude on the part of young women. Many of whom cannot yet reach far into the professional job area and are striking out in other directions instead.

Yet their apparent rebellion still may involve spending heavily on fashionable and stylish clothing to attract the attention of the males.

Some deny this and feel that by 2005, the increasing numbers of young women who dress in ways that look outlandish often do so to compete with each other and to be ultra-fashionable rather than to attract males. Indeed, many males may be put-off by the chosen rather extreme gear.

By 2000, with the economy still sluggish and unemployment rising, it became fashionable to wear cheaper clothing, for example from Uniqlo a highly successful chain of stores, although an item from there might often be worn along with an expensive top brand item perhaps from Armani. Such "mix and match" is common.

It is difficult to see any *sudden* change in the general male attitude towards women. It would involve sweeping alterations in the way business is conducted. For example, it would be difficult for a Japanese husband to spend more time with his family and engage in housework. In order to do this, he would have to adjust his attitude towards the firm, and to the person above him, as well as modify his feelings of loyalty to the work group. He might have to leave work before the boss, which is currently hard to imagine, or refuse to go out for a drink with colleagues, also difficult to conceive. This suggests that small adjustments, nibbling away at the edges, are more probable than a rapid and major change, for that would take a revolution in attitudes as well as behavior.

Laws and Regulations

Over-regulation abounds

Detailed laws and regulations are widespread in Japan which is a surprisingly bureaucratic society. This is accepted as normal to an extent that would probably be resisted in more individual cultures. Privacy and keeping secrets from the group are not important concepts and the idea that individuals may sometimes need protecting from their rulers is alien. All living in Japan have to fill in detailed forms for the local police station, which keeps the records.

In order to do business, you will often find that there are awkward reporting requirements that have to be met. This is part of the belief that much knowledge should be in the hands of the state and it is not designed merely as a form of protection against foreigners, although it may work to that effect. There is nothing you can do but learn to live with it.

Oddly, the law itself is not that important

Despite the regulations, the law in an abstract sense is not taken particularly seriously. Rules are followed because group harmony (*wa*) demands this.

Contracts are often ignored, or at least the words used in them are not taken seriously. This attitude towards contracts is slowly eroding as Western ideas are examined and some felt to be useful, but the general attitude persists. Many things are written into contracts because some foreigner insists on it, rather than because the Japanese company thinks it is necessary, or even a particularly good idea.

Government departments "suggest"– and people jump

Government departments are most powerful and a quiet suggestion from one almost has the impact that a law would have in Western society. A firm ignores such official advice at its peril. The state controls companies in indirect fashion, using the approach of administrative guidance. If you are operating a company in Japan, this is worth noting. By the mid 1990s, some minor relaxation of the seriousness with which official hints are taken had begun to appear, but most companies still comply immediately. The most powerful of the departments is the Ministry of Finance which does everything from drawing up the national budget, to raising taxes and supervising the financial sector of Japan. Many agree that its power is too great but, despite efforts, it is proving hard to trim back.

Orders are followed

Japanese tend to obey instructions without hesitation. They do not feel it clever or smart to get away with rule breaking, unlike say in the UK, USA or Australia where this might easily occur if it made sense to do so. In Japan, such behavior is more likely to horrify than be regarded as sensible or amusing. If you skirt the law or find an ingenious way of getting around some regulation, it would be unwise to mention this to anyone and you should *never* boast about it.

Other Cultural Features

The race issue and hierarchical ranking

The Japanese view many aspects of their own society in a hierarchical way. One area where this shows is race and there is a strong concern with racial purity in Japan. There is a powerful feeling that Koreans, Burakumin (see below, p.14) and Chinese are inferior people. The Japanese attitudes towards them are similar to those of traditional high caste Hindus towards the Untouchables in India. Over 600,000 Koreans live in Japan, having been forced or volunteered to come when Korea was a colony of Japan (1910-45), but they are usually regarded with contempt. A lot of Koreans actually look Japanese and are able to pass, but they are forced to carry ID papers at all times and are discriminated against in a variety of other ways, such as not being allowed to vote or work for the government. Even in Hiroshima, destroyed by an atom bomb in World War Two, the many dead Korean conscripts are not allowed a memorial in the Peace Memorial Park.

When a couple wish to marry, both families are likely to hire private detective agencies to investigate the background of the prospective partner. If a report is negative, it is most common for the couple to cancel their plans. In part it is a fear of contaminating Japanese blood and losing the racial purity but even in the case where the partner is one hundred per cent Japanese, there can be much anxiety about the other family's genetic heritage, particularly any mental or physical illness. The general attitude is reminiscent of bloodstock horse breeders in the West.

The Burakumin are untouchables who are still regarded with some feeling of horror and are the descendants of ordinary Japanese who were unfortunate enough to work in certain "unclean" occupations, largely concerned with dead animals. They included both those killing animals and those who used animal skins in some way, such as shoe makers. Burakumin are discriminated against in a variety of ways, including employment prospects and marriage partners, but few Japanese are willing to discuss the issue. Remember not to ask questions!

The concern with "Japanese-ness" is deep: Japanese who come from the island of Okinawa are held in some contempt for not really being true Japanese. This misgiving extends to the *Nisei*, those ethnic Japanese who are born and raised abroad. They are not really accepted, trusted, or even liked much, despite possessing racial purity. Somehow they are felt to lack some magic ingredient and are not "proper". A Japanese sumo wrestler born in Hawaii does not really capture the hearts of the masses, as he is not seen as truly Japanese. The same feeling can apply to a Japanese person sent abroad to work for the company: on their return some have found that they are not always fully accepted. Their friends tend to fear that the returned expatriate has lost something intrinsically Japanese or may have picked up some foreign characteristics which have in some way contaminated him or her. They are now too different to be fully-fledged members of the group and will probably remain something of an outsider.

Foreign countries are ranked – and some are rank

There is a clear if loosely graded hierarchy in the Japanese attitude towards foreign countries. In this hierarchy, other Asians are often disliked or looked down on, and this easily shades into hatred in the case of Koreans. The Chinese are respected for having provided the source of much of Japanese culture, but are rather despised for not having responded better to the European invasions of the Nineteenth Century, unlike Japan which immediately buckled down and set to work to catch up, and triumphed. Europeans are respected (Japan borrowed widely from them in the last century, especially from Germany) as are North Americans. The rest of the world is seen as inferior to these two groups of peoples.

On a racial basis, there is a widespread feeling that Negroes are mentally backward and somewhat inferior as human beings. Prime Minister Nakasone probably felt he was commiserating with a friend when he said the intellectual level in the United States was lower than that in Japan because of the presence of Blacks and Hispanics. He was, it seems, disturbed by the criticisms made abroad of his views, and many Japanese did not find it easy to understand what the fuss was all about. It must be admitted that many Japanese are racially prejudiced and just about all are strongly nationalistic, and feel thankful that they are Japanese and not anything else. Interestingly, Japan does not allow dual nationality for any adult: one either is, or is not, a member of the nation.

Appearances are very deceptive

There is a striking difference between appearance and reality in Japan. This is inevitable in a society which places great emphasis on appearance, presentation, politeness and style, while attempting to maintain many feudal attitudes in a modern and democratic world. These old-fashioned attitudes involve strong feelings of social ranking, and include automatic obedience and loyalty to those above. These ingrained views tend to clash with more modern and Western views of equality, as well as traditional ones of group solidarity and at least some participation in decision-making. In order to reconcile possible contradictions and avoid embarrassment, everyone understands that a surface appearance must be maintained, while a different reality proceeds underneath. The words *tatemae* ((tah-tay-ma-eh), meaning "face" or the image projected to the public, and *honne* (hone-nay), meaning "real intention", are used to describe this. This split allows the complex system to work and is flexible enough to deal with rapid change.

The dichotomy between appearance and reality shows in many areas. The real holders of power are often invisible, even at the highest levels of the nation. In most major companies meetings of staff are constantly held to discuss issues and reach a decision – but everyone present waits for the leader to indicate the preferred view, which they then adopt. As a different example, things may be said which are known to be untrue, but uttering the falsehood prevents someone else from losing face. Related to this, the word "yes" can easily mean "no", "maybe", or even nothing at all. When dealing with Japanese, it is easy to see the appearance but it takes time and skill to delve through to the reality underneath. Experience and sensitivity are required.

In similar vein, style, good taste and appearance are most important, often mattering more than substance. It all means that in Japan you can never accept things at their face value and you should try to think carefully about what might be the hidden meaning that lies behind the words you hear. What you are told and what you think you see may not be what you finally get.

Education is Confucian – with its attendant problems

The Confucian approach to education involves much rote learning, discipline, and emphasis on conformity. It often discourages questioning and creative thinking. This is a problem for any modern economy and the Japanese are well aware that they could do better here; there is just no agreement on how. Education is seen as serving a social purpose, such as building a national identity, and moulding the young into a desired type of adult, and not as a way of helping individuals to develop their full potential. As a consequence, rigid central control exists, even down to the level of the detailed content of the textbooks used in all schools.

There is a fiercely competitive struggle among children to succeed and climb the educational ladder to the finest universities; these are widely recognized and Tokyo University is seen as being at the top. All the institutions at each rung of the ladder are ranked, including high schools, junior schools and even kindergartens. For a Japanese family, it is important to get one's children into a kindergarten that has a good record for successfully promoting its young charges into excellent schools and ultimately to the elite universities. The child is under pressure all the way through, from teachers, peer group and parents, especially the mother. To Western eyes, Japanese children often seem to be deprived of childhood. Many suffer, and some cannot stand it and crack up; too many commit suicide under the strain.

Once at university there is an abrupt change: for most students the pressure is totally removed. It is difficult to fail, and many students tend to drift through doing little or no work, as if they were taking a holiday after the rigorous years of hard dedicated work to get where they are. For many this is a time of developing social skills and contacts. After graduation, the former students buckle down and start to work hard again.

A degree from a well-regarded university, at least until very recently, meant a guaranteed job for life, in either a large company or the public service. The recession in the 1990s weakened the likelihood of this, but parental perception has not changed; the strong pressure to force their child to climb the ladder continues.

Japan is a very safe country

By Western standards there is little crime. Street crime is particularly rare and it is generally safe to walk around all city areas, even the most sleazy, without fear. You might be seriously overcharged in a local bar but are unlikely to be physically mugged or robbed. The Japanese themselves tend to worry about rising crime levels, although there has actually been a fall in many crimes over the last few decades, in contrast with most other modern industrialized countries. Drugs are not a particular problem and until now the only real substance-abuse concerns glue-sniffing among a small minority of youngsters. The offenders are often unskilled and ill-educated, and already see themselves as having failed in life - in a land where every child is dedicated to succeeding and getting into the best university possible.

The reason for the generally high level of safety is not the attitude to law, which as an abstract concept is not particularly respected, but a mixture of things like a strong social pressure to conform, a desire not to lose face, and a wish not to bring shame upon parents and family. Another and more formal crime deterrent is the conspicuous presence of neighbourhood policemen who are very familiar with the area and its residents. Local police stations are widely scattered throughout urban areas.

A robust sense of local community is also a deterrent against crime. Neighborhood Associations are common and function effectively as a group binding agent. Strangers stand out and people tend to keep an eye on them. The neighborhood organization may also maintain a system of a sort of civilian "Duty Officer", to whom people can report any problems. In addition, there is a widespread urban public-address system, with loud speakers mounted on poles, which issue frequent announcements from a local municipal office; this helps to build a sense of community and also strengthens local control. In general, the older areas enjoy a greater sense of community than the multi-storey blocks of flats and the sprawling commuter belts.

Shame on you!

Shame is taken far more seriously in Japan than in the West. As an example of the seriousness with which shame is regarded, the parents of some Japanese Red Army terrorists actually committed suicide. As another example, in Japan, a manager may choose to punish an underling merely by staring hard at him or her. This actually works and the person would feel humbled and ashamed. Finally, the behavior of Kamikaze pilots in the Second World War, when they were prepared to face certain death to help the common cause, never fails to amaze Western observers. The horror of the shame involved if they failed to hit the target, even when it meant dying as a result, lurked underneath the more positive feelings of obeying the dictates of group loyalty and sense of face.

During negotiations, you might find the Japanese side tries to shame you into making concessions as it works for them and they may think it will work on you.

For working spaces, small is beautiful

Land is expensive and observing senior executives sharing an office is quite common. However, they will usually only share with someone of the same status; the all-pervasive hierarchical view of society prevents those above dealing equally with those below. It is common to see several vice-presidents in one tiny area, whereas in the West, each would probably insist on having his or her own rather splendid office. This sharing of working space has the benefit that people know what their colleagues are doing and information passes quickly and easily between people. The notably high noise level that results does not seem to cause a problem for most Japanese, who have perhaps got used to it in the small, cramped dwellings in which many live, and their unusually heavy involvement in watching TV and listening to the radio.

Homosexuality is not discussed

Homosexuality has been tolerated in Japan, but it was never considered a fit topic for discussion and until recently was kept underground. A change is under way and back in the summer of 1994 the first-ever gay parade by lesbians and gays was held in Tokyo. AIDS is still not something that is openly discussed and it is often presented as solely a disease of foreigners. It is known that hospitals frequently do not inform sufferers with HIV that they are infected but because condoms are widely used in Japan (contraceptive pills are banned), AIDS has not spread quickly. You are unlikely to face a discussion about AIDS, but if it arises, you should not be surprised if foreigners are blamed for the whole thing! You might feel that polite sympathy is in order.

Public "bad manners" can contrast sharply with private politeness

For some reason, certain acts are more tolerated in public than in private which strikes some Westerners as very strange. For example, if you live in Japan for any period of time, it would be unusual not to have seen some man urinating or vomiting in a public place. This would be regarded as disgusting in most Western countries, but such behavior is regarded as reasonable in Japan, as long as it done is in a public place and not, for example, in someone else's garden.

Drunks occupy a special place in the culture

Many Japanese seem to regard them tolerantly or with some amusement, even when they are rowdy. A sort of "stage drunk" appears in quite a few Japanese movies and despite the character being unreliable, untrustworthy, or possibly a thief, he is normally presented in a humorous and understanding manner.

It is acceptable, probably desirable and really inevitable that you become drunk while doing business in Japan. When you are invited into a Japanese group and they are drinking heavily, you are expected to do the same. Under such circumstances, not to join in enthusiastically would be to let the side down and do your reputation considerable harm. Some of the drunks you will see in the street are highly respectable businessmen on their way home after a social-business session with the boys. They are not the lager louts of some Western societies or skid-row residents with a bottle in a paper bag staggering along looking for a doorway to sleep in.

The name of the Emperor

You might sometimes encounter a blank look if you refer to the current or any earlier Emperor by his name. This is because when a Japanese Emperor ascends the throne, he always chooses a name for his ruling era, and the counting of his reign starts with "Year 1" of that era. An occasional pause before you get a reply is because Japanese think of and refer to the name of the era rather than the Emperor as a person. When an emperor dies, he loses his own name and henceforth is referred to by the name of the era. The deceased Emperor Hirohito is now known as the "Showa Tenno", and not as Emperor Hirohito, because he is the Tenno of the Showa era. He was of course older than the name of the era which now refers to him.

People are generally optimistic and look on the bright side

Perhaps because of the influence of Buddhism which emphasizes impermanence and the normality of suffering, most Japanese people tend to expect progress and improvements. After a bad event, such as a building being destroyed, many will tend to say that the new one will be better and more enjoyable than the old. There is a fatalism about the culture but it is not pessimism. This shows in successive official pronouncements about the long-running recession that began in 1991 – it has been about to end an awful lot of times!

White gloves are a form of polite dress in some occupations

You will notice workers such as airline pilots, many police officers, bus and cab drivers, all staff working on trains and some politicians wearing white gloves. These are considered to be a badge of cleanliness, purity and professional respectability. Many of the heroes in *manga* comics and action video games are also depicted wearing them, presumably to look smart.

Two: Some General Advice

Be sensitive to the culture – save time and make money

An understanding of the culture will pay handsome dividends by allowing you to develop faster relationships and in this way achieve quicker and better results. Before going to Japan, it would be valuable to read a book or two about Japanese culture and history. In discussions, someone might mention things such as the Meiji Restoration: all those present will understand the allusion, examine it as a possible parallel situation, and pick up the message. Without such knowledge, you may remain in the dark and flounder, trying to understand what is in their mind. If this occurs, it will be clear to the Japanese that you know little about their country; they will then see you as rather uncivilized and perhaps not worthy of trust or a suitable person with whom to do business. Helping you is the fact that the Japanese feel they are unique and therefore do not expect foreigners to understand them well anyway; a little knowledge on your part is always extremely useful and rarely a dangerous thing.

Politeness pays

Japan is a nation that takes politeness very seriously and you should try to conform to their view of what makes up good manners. When dealing with the Japanese you will find an awareness and use of Japanese etiquette to be a quicker and easier route to success than simply doing what you would normally do. If you learn a few polite phrases, and behave in a polite Japanese way, people tend to be impressed and warm to you quickly.

More than in most countries, there are lots of things that should be done, and others that should not be done, simply for politeness' sake. Style, outward form, and "proper" behavior are drilled into children from an early age and any deviation from polite behavior is curbed, as is any individuality of expression. In Japan, there are rules for doing all kinds of normal daily things that have probably never occurred to you as mattering, and so you do them in your own individual way. Because foreign ways are usually different from the accepted Japanese version, the Japanese have learned to regard virtually all foreigners as being "bad mannered". On the plus side, as you will recall, most Japanese tend to accept your rude behavior because they know it is not your fault; you are unlucky enough to have been born foreign. Apart from that, Japanese ways are widely felt to be just too sophisticated and difficult for a foreigner to understand and follow properly.

Safe topics for all occasions

You need to know what are safe topics of conversation, and then enough about the issue to be able to keep your end up. It is necessary for two reasons. First because preliminary social chatting is a must before any business can be done and secondly because when out drinking and dining with their team you need to be able to join in wholeheartedly and exchange views. Demonstrating a degree of knowledge about Japan will impress the person that you really are interested and by revealing knowledge of the culture you are showing that you are a hardworking person and have done your homework. This helps to develop a bond and builds a productive business relationship more quickly.

In Japan, there are many safe topics and relatively few taboos.

Table 2.1 Safe topics of conversation

The aging of the Japanese population	Japanese paintings
Japanese ceramics	Japanese poetry
Japanese culture	Japanese theatre
Japanese education	Local shopping centers
Japanese flower arranging	Restaurants
Japanese food	Sports
Japanese history	The weather
Japanese landscape gardening	Urbanization effects

The weather always provides a good topic and if you live in Japan, it is almost expected that you will start with this. The weather is generally going to be rather unpleasantly hot, cold, wet, or muggy, depending on the season! A respectful and sympathetic approach, perhaps enquiring how the other person is coping, is essential, and you might avoid jokey phrases such as "Hot enough for you?" If you are a visitor, you might face polite enquiries about your journey to Japan, which hotel you are staying in, or your impressions of the country.

Japan has a low birth rate and the highest life expectancy of any country in the world which means the population is ageing rapidly. Pensions are inadequate to live on and yet most men are forced to retire at fifty-five or sixty. The willingness of urban youth to take care of parents is declining and there is a real problem of increasing numbers of aged poor. This is a serious cloud on the economic horizon and in the future it could force a major reallocation of resources towards the old. The Japanese often discuss this issue with particular attention to "Will the youth reverse their current attitudes and accept the duty of parental care?" Some worry also about the possible worsening of labour shortages. If you are in Japan for long, you can expect this topic to appear at some stage.

The problems of Japanese education are an acceptable talking point – this topic is dear to the heart of many. If you are in a restaurant, asking about the Japanese names for the plate, fork etc., is often a good way to open the conversation with your business colleagues and you will probably find them eager to instruct you. You will discover that many of the words are based on the English. Sport is a reasonable issue to discuss and many Japanese are interested in baseball, which was introduced by Americans in the last century and caught on as a national sport, although its popularity has waned somewhat since the 1990s. The Giants are the best known local team. Soccer has become something of a recent fad and children kick footballs around a lot these days. Golf is a good topic also. Japanese films are usually worth discussing and a mention of any one will go down well. If you are interested in judo, karate or sumo wrestling, or tried out a martial art when young, it might prove a fertile and bonding topic of conversation. It is a good idea pick up a local English-language newspaper as soon as you arrive and study it to see what is going on. This will give you a few topics of current interest that you can discuss.

Table 2.2 below provides enough information for you to ask some intelligent questions. It is best to use the information as a way into getting them to talk rather than to pretend to know about the issues, because your lack of depth would instantly be recognized. Even if you have genuine knowledge, it would be polite to hide this at first – the nature of your questions will reveal it to them and you could lose brownie points if you sound too knowledgeably arrogant.

The "instant expert" table of arts below (Table 2.2) allows you to drop a few names and ask about them, which demonstrates interest and cultural awareness. You should not try to bluff with information unless you have seen or read something about it i.e., you have real knowledge. The Japanese are very good at detecting insincerity and weakness.

Table 2.2 Some art information to help in discussions

TYPE	COMMENTS
Movies	Director Akira Kurosawa (1910-98). Venerated in Japan where he is known to film-buffs as "The Emperor". He is the best known abroad of all the post war directors; the brilliant *The Seven Samurai* was remade as the western *The Magnificent Seven* and again later as the sci-fi *Battle Beyond the Stars*, while his *Yojimbo* was remade as *A Fistful of Dollars* and sparked off the entire Clint Eastwood spaghetti western series. Personally, I like the Zatoichi movies, about a totally blind itinerant masseur swordsman.
	Toshiro Mifune (1920-97) a well known actor. He appeared in many well loved films including *Yojimbo*, *Rashmone* and *Throne of Blood*, which was based on Macbeth. He also worked in international films, for example *Grand Prix*.
	Kiyoshi Atsumi (1928- 96) is a famous comedy actor; he made 48 films with the general theme of "It's hard being a man", playing a bumbling scallywag.
	Takeshi Kitano is well-known and multi-talented. He acts, makes films, and also directs seven TV shows as well as writing four magazine columns each week! You might have seen him in *Merry Christmas Mr. Lawrence*, as the cheerful Japanese sergeant playing opposite David Bowie.
"*No*" or "*Noh*" theatre	Traditional theatre using music and slow moving mime; the characters wear masks and brilliant costumes on a fairly bare stage. Sombre music gives it an almost religious atmosphere. Highly regarded as an art form.

Kyogen theatre	Largely comic farces, with stock characters like a shrewish wife and henpecked husband. Aimed at the common people, it has simple story lines which are easy to understand.
Kabuki theatre	Dramatic stories using music, dance and stupendous display to dazzle and entrance the audience. The costumes and make-up are extremely vivid.
Literature	Murasaki Shikibu, an 11ᵗʰ century lady-in-waiting to an empress, wrote *The Tale of Genji*. It is widely regarded as the greatest work in Japanese fiction.
	Mishima Yukio (1925-70) was the first Japanese writer to be internationally recognised. An extreme right-winger, he is also famous for committing ritual suicide in the traditional samurai way.
Poetry	Simplifying rather: *Haiku* are 3-line unrhymed stanzas with 5, 7, and 5 syllables respectively; they became more widely known in the West after a James Bond book included them. *Tanka* are 5-line unrhymed stanzas of 5, 7, 5, 7, and 7 syllables.
Antiques	*Netsuke* – a small carved ornamental toggle, used to fasten pouches to the sash of the *kimono*, which needed hanging purses as it had no pockets.
	Porcelain typically has rich colors on a whitish background and was traditionally favored by the upper classes.
	Pottery uses rough simple designs and was influenced by Zen principles. It is used in the tea ceremony which demands an austere and elegant simplicity.
Paintings	Chinese-style landscapes showing the relationship between a towering beautiful nature and puny man are highly regarded.
Music	Mostly favors melody lines with little attention to harmony; the *koto* (like a zither and once rather an upper class instrument), the *samisen* (like a 3 stringed banjo and more a middle or merchant class instrument) and the biwa (like a lute) are the main traditional instruments. Drums, gongs and flutes were also widely used.

Wood Block Prints	The oldest are Buddhist texts from c.770 AD which are believed to be the oldest printed texts anywhere in the world. The 17th C. saw the art form flourish when Hisikawa Moronobu (c1625-c1695) developed wood block printing with figures. In the 18th C. landscapes dominated.

You might find it useful to be able to discuss a few of the main social concepts in the culture (see Table 2.3).

Table 2.3 Some important cultural concepts

Amae ("ah-ma-eh")	"Dependency", but with no negative feeling. It describes the relationship between people, and has been described as the glue that holds Japanese society together. People see themselves as enmeshed in a set of relationships. Favors are both given and received, in business and in ordinary life.
Giri ("Ghee-ree")	The sense of obligation that one feels which obliges an *on* (see below) to be honored and repaid when demanded.
Honne (hone-nay)	One's true feelings (c.f. *tatemae*)
Kao ("Cow")	Face or self-pride; it is important not to cause people to lose face.
Ningen kankei ("Ning-geng karng-kay")	Means a group with a similar interest or background (e.g., from the same university) that engages in mutual support. In feudal agriculture, cooperative systems and mutual assistance teams were common, and the habit has persisted. There are many such groups in Japanese society and it is difficult to succeed without being a member.
On ("Own")	An obligation that someone owes to you (or vice-versa) as a result of some favor done in the past. It is desirable to obtain an *on* with someone, because in the future you can call on them and they must repay it.
Sempai-kohai (sem-pa-ee ko-	Refers to the relationship between an elder (superior, more powerful) and a younger person.

high")	The elder is supposed to give advice, loosely train, and look after the interests of the younger, as a protector. This relationship is found in schools, universities, government departments, business firms etc. If you are running a firm in Japan, you should take note of it and use the system to gently give advice. If a junior needs correcting, a quiet word to his "protector", if you can locate him, would be a good way of improving the junior's behavior.
Tatemae (tah-tay-ma-eh)	The public face or image projected for others to see (c.f. *honne*)

Unsafe topics that are better avoided

There are not many bad topics of conversation in Japan, but it is not particularly desirable for you to raise the following subjects (Table 2.4). If your host does of course then it is different – but you will find that few hosts will.

Table 2.4 Topics that are better avoided

The American Occupation after World War Two	Japanese protection of industry and commerce
The Emperor and his role	Politics
"Comfort women" in WW2	Religion
Japan and WW2 generally	Sex

Do a favor whenever you can

It is important to try to do small favors for people with whom you do business. In Japanese culture, any small favors *should* be repaid and large ones *must* be.

Even a tiny courtesy such as lighting someone's cigarette carries a small feeling of an obligation incurred. The Japanese appear to carry a small computer in their brains which records all obligations owed and owing in their daily existence. If you try to do things for business people, they may feel that they have to repay you in some way in the future – every little helps!

Living and Moving About

It's expensive over there

Expect to find Japan and Tokyo in particular an expensive place to visit or live. This is partly the result of many people being squashed into small coastal strips with a resulting high price for land and buildings, which is then passed on to consumers. The pressure on land has been intensified by the high degree of protection for farmers which has meant much land is retained in agriculture and held off the building market. Other than land, the sheer size of the economy and levels of wealth have forced up prices generally. The social preference for demanding perfection irrespective of price, which only began to weaken in the early 1990s, adds to demand pressures. Finally, for years the economy was protected against foreign competition which meant only limited availability of cheap imports, although this situation began to change, again in the 1990s. Over time the yen has tended to be a strong currency so that your own currency will often not stretch far.

If you stay for any length of time in Japan, the 100 yen stores are a particularly cheap place to buy a surprisingly wide range of items – and of course nothing costs more than 100 yen! These stores have enjoyed a boom since the recent but long-lived recession began.

Write that destination down

Before taking a cab, get your destination and its telephone number written in Japanese. The hotel clerks will be happy to do this for you. As in many countries, the cab drivers do not speak good English, but literacy is virtually universal in Japan. A particular problem you will probably encounter is you will get to the general area and then the cab driver will find it difficult to locate the actual building you seek. Few streets seem to be named and the house numbering system is unusual in that it often follows the order in which the houses were originally built. As an example, number 15 might directly follow number 96 and number 17 might not even be on the same street! This makes any particular address difficult to find even for a cab driver. You need the telephone number of your destination so that the driver can ring for instructions should you get close to but cannot actually locate the building you seek. You need not be concerned if in the last few minutes of your journey the cab driver stops to shout at people in Japanese – he will be asking for directions.

Cab doors can hurt

As you prepare to get in to a cab, be careful not to stand too close to the cab door. The door is worked from inside by the white-gloved driver and it can swing open suddenly and hard. There is no need to close the door after you get out, as the driver expects to do this for you from his front seat as part of his job. Do remember not to offer your cab driver a tip as this would embarrass him terribly. If you forget and offer him a tip he will normally refuse, looking extremely discomforted; you will have to smile broadly, apologize and retreat backwards a step or two with a small bow of the head.

Newspapers can be hard to find

It is a good idea to get your newspaper at the hotel. Newspapers are not generally available on sale – there are almost no newsagents or newsstands to be found and residents get their newspaper delivered to their home. If you do not get your hotel copy, you will probably miss out. If you forget to pick one up and get desperate, remember that you can often buy a newspaper at a railway station.

It is best not to put money straight into people's hands

There is a tradition that money should not be passed from person to person directly, and when buying something on normally places the money in a saucer or other receptacle from whence it is removed. Any change is then put back into the saucer for you to pick up.

If you get lost

Most people are prepared to help the foreigner when he or she gets lost – in fact strangers will often escort you to your destination, even if it means their going well out of their way. It is well-seated part of the culture and it often comes as quite a pleasant surprise to the tired and culture-shocked visitor.

Some Warnings

A pack of tissues could (almost) save your life

It is a good idea to carry plenty of large and sturdy paper tissues with you. Public toilets frequently have no paper, which if you are unprepared can be extremely embarrassing.

Note that in public conveniences and the lavatories on Japanese airlines it is customary to knock on the door to see if a cubicle is occupied. If it is, the person inside will knock back.

Tissues are also useful because many restaurants do not supply napkins, as you are expected to produce your own tissue and spread it on your lap. Observe that the Japanese use disposable tissues, not handkerchiefs, and they blow their nose in as unobtrusive a fashion as possible. They later discard the used tissue equally unobtrusively. It seems terribly unhygienic to them when foreigners wrap up their nasal emissions in a handkerchief then deliberately carry this around with them in their pocket all day! It has been said that they wonder what foreigners intend to do with the contents later....

Blowing your nose is indeed yuk!

You should never blow your nose in front of a Japanese person as this is considered truly disgusting. It is regarded in much the same way as raking in the back of one's teeth with a finger would be in Western cultures, or even picking one's nose.

It is considered particularly bad to blow your nose at the dining table; if you feel the need, then you should excuse yourself, go to the bathroom and do it there, preferably using a tissue rather than a handkerchief. If circumstances really do not permit leaving, then blow as quietly and discreetly as possible, half turning away as if you are trying to conceal the fact. This will still make people feel queasy but it makes it easier for those present to ignore your behavior. Honking like an elephant is of course totally out!

Rather than blow their nose, many Japanese will prefer to sniff constantly, an event that many Westerners find somewhat disgusting. If you encounter it, hide your feelings; their hostile attitude towards nose blowing is dominating their behavior. Just hope that the person sitting next to you on a Japanese airline does not have a cold as has happened to me!

A similar personal habit that Westerners will find repugnant is the Japanese male habit of poking down their ears and cleaning them in public. At least you are warned!

Sneezing is also considered impolite

If you are forced to sneeze unexpectedly, you will probably have to blow your nose shortly afterwards, so you might wish to excuse yourself immediately and head for the rest room. There is an old folk belief that one sneeze is an insult, two means you're being laughed at, three means you are being admired, and four means you are simply catching a cold! If unlucky enough to sneeze suddenly, perhaps you could mention you have heard about this, as your knowledge about Japanese culture could help to overcome the *faux pas* and help to restore harmony to the group.

Beware the ultramodern toilet

Traditional squat toilets still exist but they are being replaced by more modern ones. Should your knee joints give you problems, try to avoid the traditional type of lavatory. If you should come across a modern "shower toilet", take special care! They are a cross between a bidet and a lavatory, with lots of controls which are labelled in Japanese only. Pressing the wrong button can be painful, as the sudden and unexpected jet of water might be both powerful and hot. Another button might even provide you with sound-effects from nature, in order to cover natural body sounds.

Smoke gets in your eyes

Many men smoke in public but few women. It is common to find smoky rooms, restaurants and bars, with people lighting up without any consideration for nonsmokers. Americans in particular find this offensive as they are used to nonsmoking restaurants etc. and even Europeans, who tend to smoke more than Americans, can find it repellent. You simply have to live with it I fear.

Eating on the street is a no-no

Eating and drinking while standing or walking down the road is regarded as barbaric and, at least until recently, few locals would contemplate doing this. You might observe items such as ice-creams being consumed outside a shop however, usually by teenagers.

Crossing the street

Unless you come from Britain, Australia or a handful of other countries where they drive on the left – be careful when crossing the road. It is so easy to glance to the left looking for traffic as one steps out – but in Japan you have to look to the right! It is said that Winston Churchill met this fate when visiting New York where he received a slight injury when stepping out and looking the wrong way.

Expect to be stared at and discussed

Many Japanese do not feel inhibited about staring at a foreign person and discussing them, including their age, clothes, posture and anything else about their appearance that strikes them as different.

You might even provoke giggles about the way you look and behave. All you can do is ignore it.

Pushing and shoving

Despite the heavy emphasis on good manners, pushing and shoving are normal in the overcrowded Tokyo transport system. You might be surprised how much jostling goes on. The root of the problem is population pressure. City housing prices are high and many people can only afford to live a long way out. Commuters may have to travel up to three hours a day or more and they are in a hurry to get to work or get home. The strong social pressure to be on time, e.g., for appointments, adds to the general hurly-burly.

Small criticisms can harm your prospects

It is easy to inadvertently criticize someone's behavior which might be taken as criticism of the country as a whole. You will probably come across behavior in Japan that seems strange or even shocks you. For example, you will probably notice people wearing T-shirts or sweaters with strange, perhaps crude or obscene, English slogans (the wearer does not know what the words really mean but likes the appearance and feels foreign is stylish and dazzling). The habit of slurping noodles in restaurants grates on some foreigners. If something like this happens to you, it is best to ignore it and never criticize it, not even in a "We do it differently" way.

Asking why can be a waste of time

If you see things that intrigue you, it may be better not ask why things are that way. Cultures are complex and hard both to understand and explain; what seems to you to be a simple question may require a deep understanding of Japanese systems and ways of thought before you could grasp the answer properly. Many Japanese would probably not know where to begin to reply. It is better to just accept things are the way they are. Remember that foreigners are not really expected to understand the Japanese in any case, as most Japanese feel they are unique and extremely hard, or more probably totally impossible, for other nations to understand. Of course, if you live in Japan and have learned about the society, then you might wish to enquire as it shows a friendly interest and the desire to develop an even greater closeness with the culture.

Always seek to find something favorable to say

If you are asked what impresses you about Japan, find something nice to make a favorable comment about, not something that you found strange or bad, or conspicuously absent.

Try not to smile overmuch

To a Japanese individual, smiling is a way of displaying emotion which is considered to be bad; while smiling is acceptable in small doses, it should not be overdone. The Japanese tend to smile less than most Westerners, and considerably less than Malaysians, Filipinos and Thais. Generally, you should try to keep you mouth closed, and avoid laughing aloud. You should especially not indulge in enthusiastic laughter where you throw back your head with a gaping mouth. This would look disgusting to any well-brought-up Japanese. Unless relaxing with close friends and possibly drinking heavily at the time, Japanese have a tendency to think that only children are allowed to laugh aloud if something amuses them - adults should have grown out of it.

You should not assume that every smile you receive means friendship. In Japanese culture, a smile can be encouraging, but it can also show shyness, acute embarrassment, discomfort, regret, or even irritation and anger. Japanese tend to find it hard to cope with any unexpected or strange (to them) behavior; as a result they may smile or laugh at things that are in no way amusing. This seems to be a nervous reaction, which reflects embarrassment, and has nothing to do with the humor of the situation. Some Western WW2 prisoners reported that they were horrified by Japanese guards smiling at extremely painful events – yet in many cases these smiles would reflect horror and embarrassment about not knowing what to do, rather than indicating enjoyment. The captives interpreted the smiles in their own cultural way and were unable to understand this facet of Japanese culture.

Beckoning is done differently in Japan

It is probably better never to beckon anyone at all, but if you ever need to do so, you should not beckon in the normal Western way, with the palm uppermost and crooking a finger. The gesture is not used in Japan. If you must beckon someone, keep the palm turned downward and beckon underhand, crooking your fingers and waggling them. This is the normal Japanese way of doing it and will at least be understood. The Japanese beckoning sign looks very similar to a Westerner waving good-bye so be careful not to confuse the two.

Group behavior can seem bad mannered

You might on occasion see group behavior which seems ill-mannered, especially if they are socializing. Groups of male Japanese go out drinking and carousing in the evening as a matter of course. They can be noisy and boisterous, especially towards the end of the evening. Not only will they probably be drunk but they tend to see strangers as outsiders who are often considered to have no rights and deserve little respect. You are unlikely to be personally insulted, as foreigners in Japan are rarely treated badly.

Public criticism is a major humiliation

During negotiations, try to express yourself smoothly and avoid putting someone down at meetings. Criticizing someone publicly to their face is a horrible insult in Japan and if you do this you would probably make an enemy for life.

If you ever need to criticize a Japanese staff member, and you happen to be in public, the way to do it is actually to praise them, but faintly, then afterwards see them on their own. At the private meeting you should start by praising their behavior etc., again, and then suggest how they could improve it even more in various ways. This will be understood both as an order to improve themselves and a criticism, but you have done it in an acceptable and proper manner.

Fake feelings are rapidly detected

Although there is a strong need to build up relationships in Japan, these must be genuine. Never try to fake a relationship. Japanese society uses indirect communications and a series of complex messages get passed in code. Japanese wish to hide emotions and avoid anything that might cause conflict or group disharmony, which results in them presenting a bland face to others. All their lives, people are steadily engaged in an effort to decode situations and detect the reality behind the superficial mask. They have had much practice at trying to discern real feelings and attitudes and their ability to recognize a fraudulent friendship is consequently high. If a member of your delegation or staff is prejudiced against foreigners generally, or against the Japanese as a nation, that person is definitely not suitable for work in Japan.

You should never patronize a Japanese

Their feeling of innate superiority, as a nation and race, means that any suggestion by you that they or their country is in some way inferior is extremely hurtful. Even a trace of a patronizing tone by you is likely to be recognized at once for what it is and they will downgrade you and your company, of which you will be felt to be a typical member.

Ethics, schmethics

While in Japan, you might encounter an example of what seems to be quite unethical behavior or blatant corruption. There have been cases of staff of internationally reputable Japanese companies engaging in industrial espionage in the USA, as well as in Japan. There been several scandals involving high level politicians taking substantial bribes from domestic and foreign businesses, the most famous being the Lockheed scandal of 1983, when Prime Minister Tanaka was found guilty in court of accepting bribes amounting to 500 million yen. Another was the Recruit Cosmos scandal of 1989, which involved politicians accepting cheap shares in a real-estate company in exchange for favors, and finally forced Prime Minister Takeshita from office. In 1994 it was revealed that an "auctioneers ring" existed in tendering for Japanese foreign aid projects, with the Japanese firms colluding in their bids and in this way ensuring high profits, while foreign firms were precluded from tendering. Not all in business and politics is honest and true.

In Western business culture, a high ethical standard and scrupulous honesty is certainly not as common as it might be; the reason is normally the pursuit of money, power or status. In Japan these drives also operate but in addition the strong belief in loyalty and protecting the group at virtually all costs adds to the pressure.

It is not really about principles

In the West, the concepts of good and bad are seen as deriving from moral principles which are laid down somewhere and there is often a sense of guilt or sin involved. The ethical situation in Japan is different: there is no feeling of either principles or sin. Good is any action that supports group harmony and maintains loyalty to superiors, including to the company and Japan. The idea of bad is the opposite, for instance whatever disturbs harmony within the group becomes a bad thing.

To many in the West a straightforward lie would be regarded as wrong, although perhaps deliberately misleading, dissembling or obfuscating would be acceptable; in Japan telling a lie can easily be a good thing to do, if for instance it promotes harmony. Many Japanese prefer to tell you what they think you wish to hear and would therefore lie to protect you rather than tell you what they see as a hurtful truth.

Sometimes commitments are given which they know are not going to be kept, but there is no feeling of guilt involved in this.

To some, foreigners are fair game

To some Japanese business people, foreigners seem to be fair game and they might deliberately mislead nonJapanese and behave in unscrupulous ways which might shock you. They would not behave like this with a fellow countryman, but apparently feel that foreigners really deserve no better. If you can build up a long-term relationship with a Japanese company and colleagues, then you are most unlikely to be subject to this; it tends to be reserved for the one-off deal with newcomers, to whom it may be felt fairness or honesty is not necessarily owed. These cultural differences suggest that when dealing with an unknown Japanese company for the first time you should be on your guard and take extra care

When not to go to Japan

It is better not go to Japan in December (and up to January 5th) or in July-August if possible. These are important holiday periods. New Year's Day is the big holiday in Japan, comparable with Christmas in Christian Western countries. Before New Year's Day, houses must be cleaned and decorated, and special foods are prepared. In July and August many people go back to their family places and engage in the traditional ancestor duties of the Shinto religion. If you go to do business at that time of the year, people will often be unable to see you. If you wish to travel, either on business or to do some sightseeing, the trains are likely to be crowded then. In any case, the weather in Japan in August is often miserable, with heat and high humidity which are worth avoiding if you can. Should you have to be there in the sticky part of the summer, and can find someone to do business with, remember that it is considered polite to enquire about a person's health and how they are coping with the hot weather.

Health Issues

You need have few worries about health treatment

If you are unfortunate enough to become ill while in Japan, you should have no worries about medical technology or the standard of health treatment, both of which are high. Unfortunately, so are the charges, so that full medical insurance is recommended.

All decent hotels can put you in touch with an English-speaking doctor. One thing you might be uncomfortable with is that Japanese doctors are rarely friendly to their patients and you might find them somewhat remote. They do not normally explain things to their patients, as they are the superior in the mutual relationship. If you dare to ask what he is prescribing for you, he might say "pink pills" – or something similar!

Probably in order to maintain harmony and avoid distressing the patient, it is common for a doctor not to tell someone the truth, even if they are dying. Many feel it is better to conceal reality in order to make the person feel better in the limited time they have left.

Patients place immense trust in their doctor, who is supposed to act in the best interests of the patient, and rarely do people think of querying their physician. Asking for a second opinion would be a grave insult, as it tacitly impugns the doctor's capability by implying a mistake might be being made. You might bear these attitudes in mind and consider if, should you become seriously ill, you might prefer to fly out if still well enough.

But bring your own medicines

All medicines you need should be brought with you. Drugs are expensive in Japan, in part because the doctors run clinics or shops that fill their own prescriptions – at a high price. In any case you will probably find it difficult or impossible to buy your particular brand of tablet in Japan, because brand names often vary internationally, and the packaging will probably be different, as well as printed entirely in Japanese.

If you suffer from hay fever or allergic rhinitis you have a particular problem as you must avoid sneezing and nose-blowing in public. You should take plenty of your usual antihistamine pills. Tablets that do not make you sleepy are preferred; remember also that you will be expected to join in drinking sessions in the evening and normal antihistamine tablets can react badly with alcohol.

Other things worth bringing with you are deodorants, shampoos, extra contraceptive pills if being taken (remember that your stay might get extended), and spare razor blades if you wet-shave.

Money and Behavior

A non-tipping society

With only very few exceptions you must never tip people. Japan is not a tipping society and indeed the practice is regarded as rather insulting, as it suggests that the quality of the performance of the person would be much lower if there were no reward. People that you are used to tipping in the West, for example, cab drivers or restaurant waiters genuinely do not wish to be tipped and will be both surprised and insulted if you try. With acute embarrassment they are likely to refuse and then not know what to do. The only exceptions to the no-tipping rule are that you should tip porters at rail stations or airport (but there is a flat fee rather than a tip at Narita airport), waiters in the sumo stadiums, rental car drivers, the hairdressers in Western-style hotels, and the cloakroom attendant in some expensive nightclubs.

Midnight cab boys

After midnight, if you want a cab you have to pay more than the amount shown on the meter, but you cannot do this by tipping. What you must do when you wave down a cab on the street, is hold up the number of fingers you will multiply the amount shown on the meter. Two fingers indicate that you will pay double the amount shown, three fingers means three times and so on. Do not simply raise your arm with your hand open as you might do in the West or you are unknowingly offering to pay five times the meter amount, and you will probably have an embarrassing argument when you arrive at your destination! It might not be a good idea to offer to pay four times the rate because holding up four fingers is seen as rather derogatory. It can be used to indicate someone is a *Burakumin*, perhaps because they used to work with animals with four legs.

To insult a shopkeeper, count your change!

You should not count the change you receive in a store. This is particularly so if you go there with Japanese with whom you hope to do business. In many Western nations, children are often instructed to count their change to make sure that it is correct and to avoid being deliberately or inadvertently robbed. In Japan, however, children are taught *not* to do this because counting change is considered to be exceptionally rude. It indicates that you do not trust the other person: when you do it directly in front of them, you are accusing them of being dishonest and in public too! This is all part of the superficial appearance but with the messages that show the hidden reality that constantly occurs in Japanese culture. You can safely assume that you will be given the correct change in Japan, for it is an important part of the social mores.

Bargaining when buying retail is not allowed
    If you offer a lower price it implies that the shopkeeper is dishonest; that you have recognized the fact that he or she is a crook; and, even worse, you are now accusing them of it to their face. Such an offer on an item would cause extreme embarrassment, they would feel insulted, and probably not know what to reply or do. They might then smile or giggle and, if they are female, put their hand over their mouth but this has nothing to do with humor.
    This advice applies only to shop customers and you must of course bargain when negotiating business matters. At the wholesale level in Japan, and when buying internationally, the Japanese have always bargained hard over prices.

Chatting with shop assistants is regarded as weird behavior
    When shopping in stores you should not try to converse with the assistants; for example it is wrong and will embarrass them if you try to discuss the weather, tell them why you are buying the item (for a present for your wife etc.) or ask their opinion about how you would look wearing the item. It would also embarrass any Japanese friend you have with you. The role of the assistant is seen as to serve, not to act as a temporary friend of equal status.

It is not done to query bills in nightclubs, etc.
    You will frequently be presented with a mere total on the bill, without any itemized breakdown or explanation, and it will often look incredibly high to Western eyes. In many cities of the world, such an action would immediately suggest that you are in a clip-joint and are being robbed. Tokyo, however, is an expensive place, and the prices in nightclubs and high-class restaurants, which are frequented by business people on generous expense accounts, tend to the astronomical. If you query a bill you imply dishonesty on their part and this insults the honor of both the person and the institution concerned. In contrast with most countries, great pride is taken in not ripping people off. The bill, although high, will almost certainly be correct. It is of course particularly important not to query the bill when in front of the people with whom you are trying to do business. They would feel that you are a clod – and even worse, they might feel

that you were insulting the whole Japanese nation, including themselves.

Stay out of new bars when on your own

You should not wander into a small bar on your own, but need to be taken by a Japanese friend who knows the place. In Japan, the entire system of bars is very different from those in Western countries. Many bars are not open to the public, even though they appear to be, and in effect they function as private clubs. If you go alone into such a private bar, you may be refused service, although the management will probably find it hard to explain why. If this ever happens to you, you should smile, bow and leave immediately. It is more likely that you will in fact be served but charged a ludicrously high price for a drink – this is to ensure that you never come back! The behavior is not xenophobia, for a Japanese who wandered into such a bar out of ignorance would be treated in exactly the same way. The actions of the bar manager is not considered dishonest in Japan: no one has lost face and harmony has prevailed, despite you having made a mistake and entered where you were not wanted. Hotel bars are of course safe and acceptable venues where this will never happen. Sticking to hotel bars when on your own may be boring, but could prove less embarrassing and expensive!

Do not drink and drive

Drunk-driving is a very serious offence in Japan and is punished severely. Further, in Japan the term "drunk" means the slightest trace of alcohol in the blood stream, not some amount deemed to be unacceptable by a Western government. In any case, if you are a visitor you may not be used to driving on the left, will probably not be familiar with Japanese street patterns, and will find that the building numbering system is definitely eccentric, so it is difficult to find your way about. Parking is pretty near impossible around Tokyo anyway, so you are far better off taking a cab, subway or train.

"I'll drink what you're having"

While drinking with Japanese business acquaintances, it is a good idea to drink what they drink. This is not because you do not know what to order. In Japan it is a common social practice to order what others are drinking or eating. It has a strong bonding effect and most Japanese feel comfortable in groups of like-minded individuals. If their leader orders beer, it is particularly important not to ask for something stronger, such as a spirit, as it might be interpreted as a "put down" or calculated insult. Many Japanese spend a lot of time looking for indirect meaning and messages and it is terribly easy for you to innocently pass along a totally unintended message.

The red-faced drinker

You might notice some of your Japanese counterparts turn red when drinking. This is common, because it is said that many Japanese men, carry a genetic variation of a liver enzyme that is less efficient at getting rid of alcohol although some experts deny this. For some unlucky people, even a small whiskey can turn their face bright red. Early contact with European sailors or colonists, who were often sunburned that color, suggested to many Asians that they must be consistently drunk! If you notice any Japanese colleagues turning red when socializing, it is better to pretend not to notice. Be very careful not to make a joke of it or suggest they cannot drink alcohol, as this would involve a major loss of face for them and probably make an enemy for you.

Other Matters

A noisy complaint is a bad complaint

Whatever the provocation, you should not complain noisily or make a fuss. The thing to do is to smile softly and ask nicely for what you want. Demonstrating antagonism and expressing emotions is regarded as impossibly bad behavior. You would be seen as a barbarian, even when what you are asking for seems reasonable. In future, that person may well refuse to have any dealings with you, and perhaps even the entire company will reject you, as the news is likely to spread quickly throughout the entire group.

It is better not to complain at all if you can manage it. People are expected to take responsibility for their jobs, even if things go wrong for reasons completely outside their control, and not whine or grumble. If you feel that you must insist, then a small smile and a slow nod of the head when you repeat your request carries a feeling of polite awareness that things are going wrong – the smile is not a humorous thing.

Apparent ignorance can sometimes be bliss

It is often desirable to pretend not to understand what is happening, even if you think you know. Partly this is because you may have actually misunderstood, and would be in danger of making a mistake, which could make you look silly. And as was pointed out before, the Japanese actually expect you not to understand their unique society. Sometimes they even seem to be incapable of admitting to themselves that you understand something, even when you clearly do. Furthermore, if you demonstrate that you easily comprehend a matter that they consider to be exclusively Japanese, it rather tends to shock them. It can easily look to them like boasting by an arrogant foreigner who has managed to understand a tiny part of the unique culture and has the audacity to commit such a terrible offence. It is often better to act dumb!

Three: Approaching Japan

Before You Go

You need one or more letters of introduction

Who can you get such letters from? If you already know which company or companies you wish to visit for discussions, you should obtain a letter of introduction from their representative in your country if there is one. If the company is not represented, then you can approach the Japanese embassy for a letter. If your company is small and not internationally known, then in addition to a letter requesting an introduction you should send sufficient information (annual reports, a PR video etc.) to the embassy to ensure that they understand that your company is regarded as well-established, reliable and respected.

If you have already done business in Japan and wish to make contact with a new firm, a suitable letter of introduction might come from the Japanese firm with which you have previously done business or perhaps a Japanese bank that you used. You could get a letter from a highly placed Japanese bureaucrat, or as something of a last resort, a representative of your country's embassy in Japan. An introduction by foreigners is normally not as good as one from a known and respected Japanese company.

Always use your letters of introduction before your first visit

Cold calling is unproductive in Japan and unsolicited letters are likely to be ignored. The Japanese tend to trust people that they have satisfactorily dealt with before and are inclined to distrust any unknown quantity that suddenly turns up. The concept of using a go-between has been around in many Asian societies for centuries, used for the arrangement of marriages as well as in business. The main idea of you being introduced by a third party is that you will be trusted if vouched for by someone who is already trusted.

Doing homework now saves you time later

It is important for you to do your homework carefully before departure. You should be up to date with the current international situation in your industry and familiar with what other countries are currently doing or talking about in your line. It helps as well if you know what is going on in Japan. The opposing team will be well-supplied with detail, and during the negotiations might come up with an obscure example to quote against you and your suggestions. You need to know enough to be able to cope, e.g., to point out that the case they instance of country X is a one-off special, caused by a unique and not particularly relevant set of circumstances. Sufficient prior knowledge can help to save you money and grief.

You should also learn as much as possible about the firms or institutions with which you will be dealing, including a bit about their history, the products they make, where their different centers are located, and how their business is currently doing.

You should also find out what you can about the individual members of their team, as well as a few of the top officials of their company. If possible, try to find any special interests of the Japanese company with which you hope to do business or sign an agreement. You might find the company has its own museum, art gallery or collection of antiques for example, or may be engaged in some noncommercial venture. The president of the company may collect stamps or have a special interest in an organization like UNICEF. Isao Nakauchi who runs the largest retail chain in Japan (Daiei) owns a baseball team and also wrote the script for a musical show! Many executives have a strong interest in some cultural area; this sort of behavior is expected of a civilized human being. If you mention such matters, it impresses their side that you are a civilized, powerful person and one they could feel comfortable with.

It also helps if you know that someone on their side has been abroad as you can mention that you are aware of this and ask his opinions about the country he visited, especially if you come from there or your firm has a subsidiary operating in it.

Demonstrating you have done some research in this way helps to convince the Japanese side that your firm is serious, worthy of dealing with, and is generally sympathetic; this can speed up the negotiating process. The gathering of such information in advance may perhaps seem alien to you and perhaps even a bit sneaky, but in Japan it is not only acceptable it is expected and seen as proper behavior. Its absence would signal a lack of hard work and proper attention to detail.

An introduction carries a definite guarantee

Bear in mind the importance of introductions and be careful whom you introduce to a Japanese business colleague. For example, it would be unwise to introduce a Western business person that you may have met casually a day or two before to a Japanese company with which you do business. If the Westerner turns out to be dishonest or lets the Japanese firm down in some way, the odium will immediately rub off on you, as the go-between involved. There is always a strong element of guaranteeing someone when you introduce them.

Table 3.1 A checklist before you go (more details below)

Have I got letters of introduction for new companies or departments?
Have I got a notebook computer with printer for daily Minutes and a built in fax for rapid communication with HQ?
Have I decided who will take the detailed notes in meetings?
Have I plenty of business cards in Japanese and English?
Is my wardrobe sufficiently formal and suits pressed?
Have I sent a list of what I wish to discuss?
Have I relearned the words of a few songs and rehearsed singing them?
Am I satisfied with all the team members?

Things to Know When You Arrive

Confirm your appointments!

Immediately after you arrive, it is important to confirm all appointments and engagements made before you left your own country. This should be done in Japanese using an interpreter to make sure that everything is set up properly. For a surprising number of Japanese there is often a sense of unreality about appointments made from outside Japan and they seem to feel the visit may not happen, so that it is important to confirm. Naturally, if you wish to alter the timetable, this is when you can suggest changes. You should however be aware that it often difficult for the Japanese to get a diverse set of people together for a meeting and if they have already set meetings up they may not react favorably to such a suggested change.

Networking your way to success

You should start to build up a network as soon as you arrive. All Japanese do this automatically through life. This network of friends and business contacts will prove invaluable to you later and will simplify your work greatly. With such a network much can be achieved; without one it is hard even to survive in business or politics. It is often possible to expedite things by using the contacts you built up in the past. Most new contacts are best made by using existing business friends and colleagues, either by a personal introduction or by means of a letter of introduction followed up by personal contact. Business in Japan is done on a basis of personal relationships.

Dealing with the Japanese

There is no substitute for face-to-face contact

In Japan there is great emphasis on personal relations. Letters, faxes and telephone calls are regarded as impersonal and are not as effective as visits at promoting your interests. You need the personal touch: the Japanese cannot go out drinking with a fax.

Strengthening the relationship

Once you have made contact you should aim to strengthen the friendship. This means meeting regularly, enquiring about the other party's health and family, and generally taking a personal interest in business contacts to a far greater degree than in most Western countries. After-hours socializing will be an important part of building up the relationship.

Why are my letters being ignored?

You must never try to rely solely on written correspondence. Not only does this not build up any rapport, you may find that your letters may never be answered. Ignoring letters is not considered to be particularly impolite in Japan, especially if it is from a stranger. You should try not to feel annoyed if your letter elicits no reply.

If at all possible, you should address your letter to a specific individual within the Japanese company; if you do not have a name, at least address it to a particular department for attention. Letters in foreign languages can easily float about for some time until someone finally decides it is too late to bother to reply and discards it.

If you are forced to make contact quickly, you will find that faxing is more effective than writing, particularly if you address the envelope in English. If you feel you really must write, and you expect to do regular business with a Japanese firm, it might pay you to obtain a rubber stamp with their name and address in Japanese. If you stamp their address on the envelope it will get delivered more quickly and a further benefit is that the small act might impress them later, because letters are usually filed with the envelope they came in. It can serve as a reminder that you may be small but you definitely try harder.

The importance of the group

It often pays to think of each individual person you meet as being an integral part of a group. There is strong identification with the company worked for, as well as with the many other groups of which a person is a member. Loyalty to others is strong and on occasion a person might act against his or her own advantage if they feel they owe the other person something. This is an important reason for working hard to build up a personal relationship with the other side.

Group loyalty can easily take precedence over principle, which means that some Japanese prefer to lie if they feel that the truth might damage the group or institution in some way. Remember that appearance and reality are often markedly different in Japan and it is unwise to automatically accept everything you are told as being gospel truth.

You should not address any Japanese by their given (Christian) name

Use of given names is far too personal and rude. First look at their card to see if they have a title, like "Director" or "Chief Engineer" – if so you should use it, ("Chief Engineer Suzuki") because this is the most polite form of address. It is not quite as good, but still polite to address people as "Mr. Suzuki" or "Ms. Atzumi", in a formal manner. Ultimately someone might ask you to call him something else but in most cases they will not.

You can also put "san" after the surname, e.g. "Atsumi-san", which is the normal form of address in Japan. "San" means something like "Mr." but has a more polite ring to it, rather like "Monsieur" in French, which has overtones of "Sir" about it. You might wait until someone else has called them "Name-san" before doing so yourself. However, you should know that if you call someone "Name-san" when they have a clear and important title, it can wound or insult them because it ignores, and therefore diminishes, their status.

Informality is the same as rudeness in Japan, it is never warranted and you will harm your cause by asking a Japanese to "Call me Fred!" Unless they are extremely westernized, they are likely to be embarrassed and unsure what to do. Most Japanese equate such informality as showing a lack of seriousness and it will reflect badly upon you.

The first name on their business card is the one to use – normally

This is traditionally their family name. However, a slight problem has recently begun to arise, as some modern Japanese have started to put the family name last on the cards they give to Westerners, in the way that we do! You may therefore occasionally face a little confusion here. It is one of the problems that can be faced if both sides learn about the customs of the other and then try to adjust to them!

Modesty is an important virtue

It is important that you be modest at all times. Japanese culture is subtle and much communication is done in an indirect and low key way. Boasting and arrogance are regarded as severe faults, whether about yourself, your product, or your company.

Even plain speaking is usually avoided as being too disturbing to harmony or even downright dangerous. In traditional Japan with its rigid social structures, acceptable behavior was rigorously proscribed for each of the different classes. Speaking one's mind freely could easily lead to summary execution for a peasant. The tradition of circumlocution and indirect speech in which something important is implied rather than openly said still persists. It means that for successful negotiating, one has to listen carefully, not only to what is said, but how it is said, and what is not said. For the really experienced, the *way* something is *not* said is also felt to have meaning! When speaking one has to avoid bragging; you should be factual about what your product can do, but preferably without comparing it with another specific product.

Strict punctuality is expected

It is crucial to be on time for appointments. Punctuality is so highly regarded that many offices still make their staff clock on or have time books which have to be signed upon arrival. It is very bad to be late for an appointment. It would indicate carelessness on your part (which is a very negative image) or else a lack of concern for the other party (which is probably worse). Many Japanese aim to be a half hour early for appointments, just to ensure they get there on time in the heavy traffic. If you do likewise, you can always find a coffee shop to wait in – there are likely to be several other people in there, sipping away and also waiting for the time of their appointment.

For purely social engagements, many countries have different habits, e.g., in England it is often felt correct to be about ten to fifteen minutes later than the specified time. You might find that a tiny minority of Japanese also feel it is smart to be a little late nowadays.

Kevin Bucknall

This is not a good policy for you to adopt. It is best to play it safe by arriving exactly on time, as this is expected, and will not shock anybody.

What to do if you are late

If you are unavoidably late, you should apologize quietly and sincerely. It is not necessary to go into long explanations as to what went wrong, as this would be considered unnecessary and indeed rather boring. To be really polite, a small bow or deep nod of head should accompany the apology. If you can convey the feeling that you are deeply sorry for having kept the other person waiting it will be of help in your relationship. Avoid a quick "Sorry I'm late!" It is important to avoid making any facetious remarks or jokes about time-keeping or how bad Japanese traffic is. This would be seen as very rude indeed.

Giving a compliment can fail if not done properly

Subtle and indirect behavior are prized. When you visit a person's office or home, it is not a good idea to compliment them directly as you might in your society. Personal praise is unacceptable and you must not say, for example, "You have good taste". If you wish to pass that message, it is better to praise something the person has around them, like a flower arrangement, or the general decor of the office (but not a particular item, see "Visiting a Japanese home" below). That would subtly indicate he or she has good taste. Because compliments are always given indirectly, it is most probable that you will receive compliments and not even recognize the fact!

Japan is not a touching society

You should never touch a Japanese person, other than to shake hands. It is important not to be over-familiar and "big" in behavior. Many Japanese are fastidious and do not like touching foreigners anyway. Backslapping, laying an arm around another's shoulder, or taking someone by the arm may appear friendly in parts of Western culture. You might even have been trained to do this in an effort to advance a relationship by showing you regard the other person as a friend. In Japan it is seen as insulting and a gross personal infringement to the individual and would do harm to your cause.

Maintain your distance to keep your friends

It is important to maintain a clear physical distance between you and any Japanese man or woman. Japanese people tend to feel happier if foreigners are kept at a distance, in part because we are simply different but also because we are often regarded as a bit inferior. Be watchful; if a Japanese person starts leaning back or even slowly moving away from you when you are talking, it means that you are infringing what he or she regards as their personal space and they feel uncomfortable. It is unlikely that they will be in a mood to agree to any of your suggestions under the circumstances. If you ever notice this happening, you should immediately retreat and open up space.

If someone retreats from you in this way, it might just mean that your body odor is becoming offensive to others, even if it is not noticeable to you. The natural body odor of Occidentals is unpleasant to many Asians. In addition, most Asians wash themselves carefully and often and so are particularly sensitive to any body odors. When in Japan, it is important to be aware of personal hygiene and to use a good deodorant and shower often. The hot, humid summers can rapidly take their toll, especially when wearing formal business clothing.

A little language is not a dangerous thing

This is not only polite and accelerates a friendly relationship, but Japanese business people are starting to expect that foreigners will know a few phrases of Japanese. If you do not speak a word of the language, a Japanese manager may privately question your commitment to dealing with Japan and suspect your long term intentions. In addition, the way a Japanese addresses someone can reveal his attitude, degree of friendship, and general intentions; e.g., there are many ways of saying "yes" or "no", with different degrees of emphasis (see Chapter 6, Tables 6.1 and 6.2, p.105). It will help immensely in negotiations if you can recognize how strongly the person opposite means what they say when your interpreter simply translates a response to you as "yes" or "of course". Furthermore, if the other team resorts to speaking Japanese language to talk among themselves, if you speak a little of the language you might be able to recognize what their problem is, or what their real position might be.

If they drop into Japanese in this way, it is important not to look bored, shuffle about, fiddle with things or leaf through your notes in exasperation. What they are doing might speed up the negotiations, as otherwise they might have to ask for a recess.

However, they undoubtedly gain a major negotiating advantage in this way, when some of them speak English but you speak no Japanese. Do not assume that you can equally exchange your views privately in English in front of them, as normally at least one of them will be fluent and listening carefully. They might even be on the team purely for that purpose. It is all the more reason for learning the language or at the very least taking your own interpreter with you rather than relying on theirs.

Introductions should be made in the correct direction

If you have to introduce people to each other in Japan, remember that generally, the less important person is introduced by name to the more important. This means that you would normally introduce a younger person to an older and a woman to a man. With two people of equal rank, consider which you wish to flatter the most and act accordingly.

Small foreign companies face a peculiar problem

The Japanese respect large companies and tend to feel that a small company, whether domestic or foreign, should adopt a rather subservient attitude with regard to bigger ones.

There is a dual economy in Japan, with a front rank of well-known large, modern industrial and commercial companies, offering great employment prospects to their staff; it is this type of firm with whom you will probably be doing business. Behind that is a second rank consisting of a vast multitude of small firms, many of which are backward, poor, and with shoddy working conditions. This second tier ties up relatively scarce labour which it uses rather inefficiently. The large companies often pass their problems down to the second tier to deal with by subcontracting out and letting them worry. When it is dealing with another Japanese firm, the more powerful company expects to get its way and inevitably seems to do so.

The respect given to large companies may be part of the general reverence for age, in that the larger companies are often older. It may also be a part of the general Japanese desire to win, be the leader, and occupy the number one position wherever they are, be it the industry, country, or the world. The winner then commands respect and much influence. It can often dictate to smaller firms but would rarely need to do this in an open fashion. Indirect methods and subtle use of influence are preferred. The small but bustling aggressive firm that is growing rapidly and pushing a bit ahead of the pack is often admired in the West. This is rarely the case in Japan. There the leaders are supposed to win and do so in a convincing fashion and establish a clear gap between themselves and the rest, not just squeak past the post ahead of a few others.

If someone flatters you, deny it!

If someone says that you understand Japanese ways well etc, the polite response in Japan is *not* to say "Thank you" or "How kind" but immediately to deny having such a skill, even if you feel that it looks slightly silly to do so.

Table 3.2 What you can say when flattered

If you are told:	You should say in return:
You do something well.	Not really! Oh no! I was trained well but my efforts fall short of what I should achieve. You (your company) do it far better.
Your company or department has done well in.....	We have really done nothing at all. Our extremely modest achievement is entirely due to the hard work of other staff.
What a lovely dinner party (etc.) you gave.	I must apologize for the restaurant (etc.) being.... (e.g. noisy, cramped, difficult to get to, looks unpleasant in the rain).

There are some things that you should avoid saying if someone flatters you

Whenever someone flatters you, and they probably will, there are certain responses which would seem normal in the West that would not sound right in Japan. There, they would seem a bit arrogant or not self-deprecatory enough. Table 3.3 (below) lists some of these.

Kevin Bucknall

Table 3.3 What you should *not* say when flattered

| You are most welcome. |
| It was my pleasure. |
| Thank you. |
| Wasn't it fun, we must do it again. |
| I'm glad you had a good time. |
| I'm so pleased you could come. |

Saying things like "Yes, wasn't it nice", as might be normal in the West, sounds rude and crude to a Japanese.

Telephone calls are peppered with interjections
Almost all Japanese feel worried if talking into a vacuum of silence, whether on the telephone or face to face. They will keep saying *hai* (yes) or some other word, perhaps *moshi-moshi* (hello), as they listen. This reassures the person at the other end and encourages them to continue. When on the telephone with a Japanese, you too will keep being interrupted in this way – just ignore it. In turn, when they are speaking, try to keep saying something like "yes", "of course", "indeed", "really", "surely" or "fine" whenever the other person makes the slightest pause. It does not commit you to anything. The same is true in meetings, where a "yes" is probably an invitation to continue and entirely lacks a feeling of agreement or commitment.

You might observe someone speaking on the phone and bowing to the person at the other end. Do not laugh! It is a structured and very polite society.

In many areas there is not a lot of competition in the Western sense
Mainstream Western economic theory assumes that the consumer is king in a competitive system and analyzes market failure as deviations from it. The Japanese approach to their economy is a little different, and attention often focuses on the producers and their wishes. This can have some odd results. For instance, despite its name, the Fair Trade Commission (FTC) has not always supported competition which would benefit the consumers. Instead, it has sometimes supported cartels, preferring market stability, and has tried to keep out new entrants in order to help existing producers. This

tends to work to the disadvantage of foreign firms trying to break into the Japanese market but new Japanese firms also suffer from decisions of the FTC. Cartels are common as is collusion in the form of group meetings, known as *dango*, to fix prices or decide who shall get the next contract by shading their price. The FTC censures firms that do this but the punishment is often minor. Competition is increasing but competition is often between groups rather than between individuals, particular within companies with separate production units or between government ministries.

"Fair competition" in Japan can have its own meaning

In the Western world, "fair competition" tends to mean having a level playing field or equal opportunities for all. In Japan the concept carries a different connotation. It is easiest understood by reference to sumo wrestling, where each fighter competes with all others, there are no weight bands to make it easier, and the small men are expected to develop special skills to compete successfully with the large. The attitude to business is similar – fair competition in Japan means "no discrimination"; if you are a smaller company, you need to develop special capabilities to survive, such as trying harder, and thinking of new ways, e.g. by offering things that the larger companies do not.

You may encounter an accusation of "excessive competition"

This will be alleged if any newcomer threatens to replace the existing leading firm which is seen as the "Grand Champion". In part, the leading companies cry "excessive competition" in an effort to maintain their power, market share, and profits. But it is more than that: a basic philosophy in Japan which underlies much behavior is a desire for harmony, stability and the maintenance of proper relationships. When a foreign firm attempts to break into the market, this will cause upsets to all existing companies and any of them might claim excessive competition, in order to preserve the natural order of things and continue to lead a simple untroubled life. There has been a clear increase in competition since the 1990s, but little change in the general antagonistic attitude towards it.

Casual clothing in Japan denotes a casual mind

Casual clothes include shorts, sandals, jogging shoes, sports gear (except when playing the appropriate sport), as well as bright colors, tartans, and all strident patterns. In fact anything but a dark formal suit is considered casual! In your own country, it may be thought smart to wear shorts, long socks, short sleeved shirts and a tie (as in

Australia) or beautifully patterned shirts worn outside the trousers (as in the Philippines). In Japan such clothing looks most strange, and is generally taken to indicate a non-serious person, who lacks appreciation of proper behavior, and is probably a rather flighty individual. If you are partial to loud sports jackets, plaid trousers, or garish ties remember these views and leave the offending garments behind. Few executives would seek out such a person with whom to do business; most would try hard to avoid doing so.

In Japan, the older you are, the more conservatively you are expected to dress. The young are allowed a little more leeway in their choice of clothing, but power largely goes with age. This means that if you dress conservatively, even if relatively young, it adds to your *gravitas* and promotes the image of you possessing power.

Only if dress standards of your own country are very conservative should you dress the way you do at home. If you are young and perhaps work in some parts of a high-technology industry like computing, you may be used to casual dress when working. If so, go out at once and buy a couple of conservative suits! You will need two suits with you, so that you can wear one while the other is being dry cleaned at the hotel. Not only does living out of a suitcase take its toll, but the sticky summer weather soon makes clothes look limp. Wearing crumpled clothing would not be well regarded and could be taken as an insult. When selecting what to take, remember that is it always better to overdress in Japan rather than to be too casual. Remember also to take plenty of dark colored socks with you – you may have to remove your shoes in public.

You can't go without an appointment!

You should always make sure you have an appointment before visiting a company in Japan. If you just show up you may be forced to wait for hours and it is probable that the people you wish to see will be unavailable. Even worse, it is possible that no one will agree to see you. Such behavior on your part would convince them that you are an ill-mannered barbarian and your company is scarcely worth bothering with.

Keep handy the details of people you have met

If you have previously met any of the Japanese team, you need their details, including family, firmly in your head. When you meet again you can refer to the earlier occasion, perhaps recall some pleasant incident together or ask after their son at university etc. This demonstration of personal awareness will help cement the existing relationship and speed up the development of new ones with any new members of their team. It can indirectly help to shorten your stay in Japan. If you have dealt before with that firm, asking after the other person's colleague is a good idea also. The first meeting is set aside for just such purposes, and you should take advantage of their system.

Do not be surprised if they know a lot about you

Even if you have never met before, the people you are negotiating with may demonstrate a great familiarity with your company, and perhaps personal details about you and your family. They may for example refer accurately to the number of children you have, where you went to university, the job you had before this one, or when you were last in Japan. Do not let this intimidate you – the Japanese have merely done their homework well. If you wish to compete equally, you will have to do the same and investigate them carefully before your visit.

The relationship between you and them is viewed by the Japanese as an ongoing flow and anything that happens is part of this, not merely an isolated incident which is unique to that particular meeting or point in time. This view of life as a continuing stream is very Asian, but it is not the way most Westerners think. If you bear it in mind, it can stand you in good stead.

The Japanese are masters of detail

They expect you to be good at details too, despite previous experience with foreigners which should suggest to them that foreigners do not conspicuously excel at such things! Most Japanese tend to respond much more positively if you can supply details immediately or produce hard facts for them. They rarely seek your opinions, or are even particularly interested in them, and always want more than vague generalizations. They wish to be given the facts, and then allowed to make up their own minds. If you have an important document which is crucial to your proposition or might have an important bearing on outcomes, it is usually helpful to read it out loud – this is not only acceptable, it is positively liked by the other team. The necessary details are being provided for them to mull over.

Things take a long time

It can take a surprisingly long time to achieve anything in Japan. You must accept that a few months may be needed to handle what seems to be a relatively simple matter. Major decisions, for example negotiating and signing an important contract, can sometimes take a year or two. Naturally it varies from case to case but if you multiply the time you might expect it to take in the West by four or even six, you might not be far out!

Why you can expect dealing with the Japanese to be a slow process

- Letters are not always answered.
- It is often difficult to get through to the right person.
- It takes time to build up a relationship and gain the trust of the other party; nothing positive happens without it.
- It is difficult to get a straight "yes" or "no".
- Gaining group agreement takes time, particularly if others have to be consulted, perhaps in another department.
- The Japanese preference for dealing with masses of details (some of which may not be required) takes time.
- Japanese tend to be cautious and want to proceed slowly.

Note that the long length of time you can expect to be involved in negotiations means that you may well need a local representative, unless you can stay in Japan for an extended period.

Response speeds are s-l-o-w

Do not expect a quick response to any proposal you make. A rapid answer is unlikely because the Japanese need to reach a consensus which takes much time. Almost all important proposals or requests for changes require clearing with several other groups of people, mostly but not entirely within the company. They have to discuss the issue and sort out any possible implications of your suggestion for their area of responsibility. This is the *nemawashi* system, or engaging in prior consultation. In most cases, written agreement to the proposal, in the form of a signature or "seal" placed on a circulating piece of paper, must be obtained from these groups, and it is impossible merely to make a quick telephone call and accept a verbal assurance. What makes it worse is that the piece of paper, called a *ringi* must go round in strict order of seniority, and if someone is not available (off sick, on holiday, abroad....) no one else has the power to sign, and it must await the return of the proper person before the piece of paper can resume its journey.

In view of the *nemawashi* system, and the likely slow progress of the *ringi* itself the team opposite is often loath to accept a radical suggestion from you, and if you make one it is likely to lead to delays. Replying to one of your letters or faxes can similarly involve a lengthy delay until the issue had been cleared around the tracks.

You might find that you attend a series of meetings and then nothing happens. The reason is of course that the results of the negotiations with you have to be circulated to all interested departments in order to secure agreement for all the details of the proposal. Few managers would dare to adopt a position before they know what the other interested groups are likely to think, so that they will delay contacting you with a reply until the decision is in.

There is not much democracy in the system

The need for prior consultation (*nemawashi*) and obtaining the signatures on a piece of paper (*ringi*) is pervasive, involves much participation, but is in no sense democratic. Discussion proceeds, with everyone being carefully indirect and ambiguous, preserving his or her own views intact, until finally the leader of the group will indicate his preference. This is then generally supported and becomes the view of the group. Quite often meetings are merely to rubber-stamp a decision made previously elsewhere. Controversial discussion of important issues is rarely done in a public forum. The numerous meetings may give the appearance of democracy in action but this is quite opposite from reality.

The Japanese want to win

They are totally dedicated to succeeding at whatever they do. This is for own their personal sake and also for their company or organization. It is crucial for them to try to become number one. In their society there is a built-in need to win, whether this means having the greatest market share locally or being the largest company in the world. They have a tendency not to do business in the ordinary sense but to wage business, in the sense of waging war. They often plan long term goals and strategies, and then work out short term tactics to adopt in order to move along the long term path and achieve final success. They are not superhuman, but they do try constantly and very hard. If you ever feel that you and they are relaxing happily together after a hard day's work, as you sit in a bar, drinking and telling stories in a convivial atmosphere, you may be wrong. More likely, *you* are relaxing and having a great time but *they* are still working, even if they are enjoying themselves at the same time.

Early Considerations

Who has the power?

You may have trouble finding out whom to approach in a Japanese company. It is rarely clear in Japan who has the power to make decisions, whether in private industries, government departments, or political parties. The *nemawashi* system diffuses authority beautifully and the sharp contrast between appearance and reality means that the person in the obvious authoritative position may actually be little more than a figurehead or perhaps a first among equals, some of whom are not in his area. Discussions go on all the time with other sections and departments within the organization, compromises are reached and agreements are made between several different groups until a final solution appears.

The fact that you cannot identify the decision maker is usually because there is no such single person in a Japanese team, nor can one team make a decision on its own. Proposals are scrutinized within the group and then passed up to other groups for consideration and finally a consensus will emerge. Who made the decision? Everyone and no one! Try not to get annoyed when it is unclear which people you should approach for decisions – this is the normal situation.

Start at the top

It is important to start negotiations at as high a level as possible but you should not rely only on top management for getting results. This level can be rather remote from activity and its function is to set general policy and not engage in nuts and bolts issues.

But put more effort in lower down

Your main effort should be at cultivating the several layers of middle-management, as that is where the decisions will eventually be made. Remember not to pin your hopes on single individuals because decisions are discussed and made in team sessions, and try to develop a relationship with as many people as you can. Someone you ignore now may have a crucial input to make at some future stage in the convoluted process; there is no way of telling.

Your early warning system

It is a good idea to advise the other side in advance what items you wish to cover. Before you leave your country you could send a memo listing all the items you want to discuss and give them plenty of detail. This would allow the Japanese to start the necessary series of meetings among themselves even before you arrive and reach a consensus on their attitudes and position. The more time saved at this stage, the faster the overall negotiations can proceed once you arrive, which helps to shorten your expensive stay.

You need to be in it for the long term

You should be looking for more than a one-off contract. The work involved in dealing successfully with the Japanese is hard and a single piece of action may not justify the effort involved. Chasing short term profits is often unwise and the effort could in damage your relationship with the Japanese company

It is vital that you convince the Japanese that you are committed to the long term. If they do not believe this, they may not be interested in your approach and reject you. There is also a danger that they may feel that what they identify as your in-and-out approach does not merit normal standards of ethical behavior and if they decide to do business with you, a nasty surprise could await.

In Japan the organic view of relationships applies also to companies; the connections are expected to start slowly and grow into something strong and binding.

Table 3.4 Your daily checklist when in Japan

Have I plenty of business cards on me or did I give them all away yesterday?
Are my clothes clean, pressed, and conservative?
Have I all the details with me that I might need during negotiations?
Am I prepared to accept a sudden invitation to drinks and dinner?
Am I ready to sing a song and swap glasses when out drinking socially?
Am I taking into account that business is ALWAYS being done and I must watch what I say?

Four: Who to Send

Why You Need a Team

Only under the most extreme circumstances should you think of going alone. Single people are not taken seriously in Japan, because in the normal run of events it is impossible for a single person to have the power to commit a company to anything at all. With the individualism of the West, we might feel that one competent person with authority is enough: in Japan they do not think like this. If you go alone, the Japanese will perhaps assume that you lack power (so they are wasting time talking to you), or are too poor or cheapskate to send a proper team (and therefore they will not wish to do business with you) are you are belittling them with a sole representative of your company. If you are a small company, two people are the minimum you can get away with, but you really need a team to impress them that you are serious. They will probably field a large team and heavily outnumber you, which if you are alone can put you at a psychological disadvantage.

You should put together a team which is as strong as you can reasonably make it. It is a good idea to take an assistant or two in addition to your functional people, because this gives you flexibility and someone to do urgent if mundane tasks. It also opens up further avenues for the Japanese to pursue in informal talks outside the meeting room. Admittedly it costs more but it can be a good investment. It is also wise to take along a technical expert, the sort of person who can handle detailed questioning off the cuff. You are likely to face a lot of this and should be able to respond on the spot. You also need a general gofer and minute-taker.

If you send a small team, one that is unable to answer detailed questions, or one that is led by someone young, then the Japanese will probably decide that their side occupies the commanding power position. They will then be inclined to feel that your team should defer to them and accept their suggestions without protracted argument. That is the Japanese way. Naturally you will not go along with this, so both teams will start at cross purposes before any details are even on the table.

Who Should Lead the Team?

A diplomat as leader

In a general sense, being a diplomat means someone who can find the correct answer quickly and present it nicely. In Japan it also means someone smooth, conservative, pleasant, rather aloof, and brimming with old-fashioned good manners. The Old English Butler as portrayed in Western film or theatre automatically tends to be regarded as a person of power by a Japanese audience. The team leader sometimes occupies a rather symbolic role, rather than being a "hands on" player. The real work is then done by those below.

Ageing leaders are respected

Age is still respected in Japan and you should try to send a distinguished looking older man as team leader.

You should not send a very young man in a leader's role; not only would he seem immature and not be trusted to deliver on promises, it might also indicate that you do not care much about the relationship you are trying to foster. In this context, "young" for a Japanese can mean anyone under fifty years of age and certainly under thirty. Anyone below that age is regarded as barely grown up and definitely too young to have much responsibility e.g. be in charge of a department. If your leader is young, many in the Japanese team will expect him to defer to them and immediately fall in with their suggestions which of course immediately weakens your team's position. What is worse, they might become annoyed when he does not do this. Further, a Japanese might easily talk down to a young negotiator and start to treat him with a degree of contempt; this would probably annoy both him and the other members of your team, and if they respond badly, both sides might be at loggerheads merely because of a poor choice of team leader.

What can you do if you are unfortunate enough to be young?

If you are young and heading your own company you have a problem and will have to make a decision. If you lead the team, you must recognize that it will harm your chances, but damn it you're the boss!

The first thing to do is to dress ultra-conservatively, like an American Senator at his most distinguished, or a member of the English House of Lords who has set out to impress. This will increase their perception of your status and power.

If you can stand the thought, you might consider putting someone older of suitable appearance and mannerisms as the official leader with a card that says "Acting President" or some such, and going yourself with a title like "General Manager". In this case the Japanese will address your leader, not you, and will expect him to make the running. You might arrange in advance that if an input from you is necessary, your team could ask for a recess in which you will be able to give him instructions. You can use a prearranged coded signal from you for your leader to request a break. This can be a clumsy way of behaving however. If you decide to adopt this tactic, do not forget that you should never interrupt your team leader, even if he does work for you! He will have to keep a discrete eye on you, perhaps for a nonverbal signal. If he does not do this carefully, the Japanese side will quickly catch on but at least they are likely to appreciate your effort to conform to their mores.

Ages and their meaning

It is worth knowing that in Japan certain ages have characteristics associated with them. This might be a useful topic of conversation when socializing in the evening after the formal business sessions have concluded. Sixty years of age is a special one, connected with the idea of rebirth. Japan, like China, has a traditional sixty-year cycle when things start again. This cycle is made up the five elements (wood, fire, earth, metal and water) each with a cycle of twelve Earthly Branches (rat, ox, tiger, hare, dragon, snake, horse, sheep, monkey, fowl, dog and pig). The age of seventy, known as "The rare old age", has special merit attached, as does seventy-seven (known as "The rejoicing age"), and eighty-eight ("The age of rice").

On the other hand certain ages were traditionally believed to have problems attached, with an added danger of bodily sickness or some special unfortunate event. For men, the age of forty-two offers the greatest threat, but twenty-five and sixty-one also have their dangers. For women, the most dangerous age is thirty-three, but nineteen and thirty-seven could also involve problems. Observe that the Japanese consider a baby to be one when born (literally the first birth day), and this difference in calculating age in Japan and the West provides a possible topic for social conversation.

Who Should Be On the Team?

Drinkers and socializers are needed

When selecting who to send, you are advised to send people who enjoy drinking and are keen socializers. Most adult Japanese males drink alcohol. This is done mainly in bars and restaurants rather than at home, and it is common to go out socializing with groups of colleagues after work. You have to be able to join in if invited: refusing such an invitation would be a dreadful insult, while going but not joining in the group activity would be seen as false and rather shameful behavior on your part. A teetotaller cannot be as effective under these circumstances.

It probably seems like mere socializing to you, but going out drinking, dining and carousing is an integral part of doing business in Japan. It is virtually impossible to wind up a deal without at least one night's drinking, singing and generally living it up noisily and two or three is common. During the process, you are being observed and evaluated. It is important to be seen as a friendly person who joins in the group, but not be considered a boisterous loud drunk who behaves badly. Remember that if you receive a written invitation to go out, it is important to acknowledge the invitation promptly in writing. You should not merely turn up on time at the right place.

It is common for adult Japanese males to smoke, and your team will spend a lot of time in smoke-filled rooms. Anyone who is allergic or who feels strongly that smoking in public is bad might not be the best choice for your team.

Men find it easier than women

Admittedly many Western women have become successful negotiators and managers in Japan, but they have to work considerable harder to achieve the same results (see Chapter 11). To send a woman would be a bit undesirable, and might actually embarrass the Japanese, as some of them would not know how to behave and would feel unsettled and unhappy. Fear of behaving improperly is a thick thread that runs though Japanese culture

If you or your company has strong views that women must not be discriminated against and you prefer to send the best person, regardless of sex, you must accept that the negotiations might take a little longer. If it is illegal in your country to refuse any position to a woman, then of course you must send her and accept it will be harder. With increased exposure to the modern and efficient Western executive who happens to be a woman, the Japanese may eventually change their views.

Fat is almost beautiful

It does no harm to send an overweight person, unless he is truly obese. In the West, the affluence and sedentary lifestyles often result in people being overweight, although slim is regarded as desirable. If you weigh more than you might wish, you can console yourself when going to negotiate in Japan. Someone with a large stomach is traditionally seen as very warm-hearted, and friendly, a bit like the traditional English "Mine Host" in charge of an inn. In Japan, the stomach was traditionally seen as central to existence, unlike in many Western countries where the mind or heart was identified as crucial to being. It was felt in Japan that a stout or even fat person might be trusted more quickly and easily. If you have something of a weight problem, it could actually help to reduce delays and speed up the negotiating process! When socializing and drinking with their team, you might even discuss sumo wrestling and express regret that, despite your bulk, you could never challenge any Japanese to a bout – as of course as a foreigner you lack all the necessary skills!

Those who went last time should go again

If this is a repeat visit to Japan, you should try to send the identical team as before, especially the same leader. The business relationship hinges crucially on the personal one and it takes a few years, perhaps up to six, to really establish a great relationship. If you keep changing your team personnel you make it harder on yourself.

Who Might Better be Left off the Team?

Extreme appearances are a no-no

You will find it easier if you do not send people such as males with ear rings or pony tails, people who dress garishly or informally, and anyone who looks casual or downright sloppy. Such a person gives an unintended but strong negative message to the Japanese that your company knows nothing or cares little about Japanese ways, and probably cannot be trusted in business. Beards once used to be a problem because the Japanese themselves rarely need to shave, so that hairy faces were considered to be either eccentric or barbaric. Times change and neatly trimmed ones now are becoming acceptable but not huge bushy ones.

Communication of status in Japan involves a great deal including the clothes you wear, the words you use, the position you occupy, and the way you stand and sit. They automatically try to read your status, and treat you accordingly, following their own principles. There is no room for the brilliantly brained but personally sloppy-looking person in business-Japan. The Japanese have never produced a Bill Gates. They always dress carefully and suitably for whatever they are about to do. In business this means formal suits, with the most senior person expected to wear the best cloth and beautifully tailored outfits. Even when enjoying relaxed private occupations, such as going for a walk in a hill park, the Japanese do not just require casual clothing but *the correct kind* of casual clothing designed specifically for that purpose. When you are on a car trip with a few Japanese friends, if you suddenly suggest stopping the car and enjoying a brief walk it would probably result in a certain amount of dismay. Your friends are likely to feel that they are properly dressed for a car ride but totally unsuitably dressed for walking on a hill! In Japanese society, one's clothing, behavior and language must always be appropriate for the task in hand.

One's position in a company affects not only the clothing worn. When promoted, a Japanese person is expected to dress differently, break most of the old horizontal ties and friendships, and use quite different words to address former friendly colleagues. Conformity is the rule in Japan and any deviation is strongly suspect. It is widely believed that there is simply a right way and a wrong way to do most things, just as in Japanese calligraphy, and blatant individuality means that you are not doing it right. Certain patterns of behavior are expected and children are schooled in these by their mothers. Girls, for example, are taught modesty, diligence, tidiness, elegance, and housewifely skills, as well as to be supportive and accept their place. Boys for their part are allowed a great deal more latitude, although they are driven to study hard.

The dark skinned

This is a difficult area to discuss, but if you wish to do well in Japan it is better not to send anyone of mixed race or who is dark skinned. They will probably be treated with a friendly tolerance but you should be aware that many Japanese will regard them as a something like a talented freak, and not to be taken seriously as a proper business person. If you wish to be politically correct and send a balanced team of your choice, that is fine, and there are limits to what one should do to try to fit into another culture. Expect however that you will have to work that much harder to achieve the same results.

You should not send anyone who is bitter about Japanese behavior in World War Two

If you send such a person, the Japanese will rapidly work this out and are unlikely to want to do business with you. It is always best not to mention anything to do with the Second World War ("The Pacific War"). The defeat by foreigners was so difficult to face that when broadcasting the surrender, Emperor Hirohito could not bring himself to say Japan had lost, but used a euphemism, saying that the stage of the war reached was "Not necessarily to Japan's advantage". Neither should you raise the issue of the Greater East Asian Co-Prosperity Sphere (which was the Japanese name for those parts of South East Asia which were invaded and occupied), the prisoner of war camps, "comfort women" or any atrocities. As you can imagine, these are incredibly sensitive topics and even casual reference to them should be avoided. Note that if the Japanese do discuss the 1939-45 war, they tend to portray Japan as a victim. The are likely to stress the extreme peril of Japan being cut off from its lifeline of raw materials and fuel, how badly Japanese were treated by foreigners, and the immense devastation and suffering that was caused by the two atomic bombs.

Also out are pushy, fast talkers and aggressive sales personnel

It would be better not to send someone who is a fast talker who tries to stampede people into agreement. Pushiness is deplored in Japan and does not work well. Anyone who makes a habit of issuing a forthright positive statement and then adding "Right?" on the end, as an easy way of carrying the argument is a bad choice for dealing with the Japanese. Not only will this person put peoples' backs up and make the task of reaching agreement harder for your team, the Japanese will probably regard him as a second rate individual who lacks real authority. It is much easier for the soft-sell expert to carry the day. Note that sending people who are good listeners can be effective. Such a team would tend to persuade the Japanese that your side is both civilized and has real authority.

Lawyers

It is still best to try not to send a lawyer to Japan as part of your team, at least on your first visit. Lawyers are regarded as a fairly unpleasant species of individual, much as they did to Dr. Samuel Johnson (1709-1784), who said "I would be loth to speak ill of any person who I do not know deserves it, but I am afraid he is an attorney". If you include a lawyer on your team, the presence strongly suggests to the Japanese that you do not trust them and that is why he is there. If your preferred team leader is a lawyer you have a minor problem. The Japanese will not like it and would probably be dubious about the whole operation as well as question your integrity. It is not likely that your lawyer could hide the fact of his training and function; and if you are a reasonable sized company, the Japanese will probably have done their research and know who the people on your team are even before you arrive in Japan. Instead of taking a lawyer, you could get your legal department to prepare a draft contract before you go, and you could fax back any Japanese suggestions for inclusion in the contract for your lawyers to look at.

In the 1990s the Japanese became a bit less antagonistic towards lawyers and some have even begun to appreciate the value of using them so that it is easier to bring in a lawyer than it used to be. Depending on what you are trying to achieve, you might benefit by using a local Japanese lawyer in the later stages of the negotiations, but it is perhaps better not to include him in the earlier ones.

The Best Use of High Level Visits

The pre-visit visit

Before the first proper business visit it would help you if you were to send a really highly placed person on a goodwill mission. His function would be to persuade the opposite party that your company is respectable, enduring, cares about developing a long term relationship, and is led by a civilized (in the Japanese sense) individual, whom one would not be ashamed to know or do business with. If your company President or Chairman is available, that is a good choice. Anyway, it will do him good to get out of the office and earn his salary on the ground! His visit is really semi-social and he must not introduce matters of business or mention money, but strive to be nice, understanding, intelligent, personable and generally impress.

For maximum beneficial effect, he should dress immaculately, look distinguished, behave like a suave diplomat, and have good deportment, with no slouching when standing or sitting. He should also have a business card that lists as many of his official titles as possible, both within the firm and outside it.

The proper work of starting the negotiations comes later and will be done by people at a lower level in both firms.

After the pre-visit, on your first exploratory trip to Japan, you should not send a subordinate

Instead, you should send a top executive who will later run the operation or at least be involved in it at a high level, whether located in Japan or the home country. The person selected should preferably be male, experienced, interested in foreign countries, intelligent, and flexible in attitude. He should not be young. You ought to plan on a minimum trip of two weeks.

At this stage you have two main aims: 1) to identify a gap in the market for one or more of your products; and 2) to assess its size.

Once you are there

After your arrival, it is important to watch TV advertisements to see what products are currently being promoted in Japan; it is a country of sudden fads and changes in style, not only in design but in a wide range of things like hobbies and sport. The women in particular spearhead new crazes, whether for French food or Philippine drinks; such fads are often short-lived. The over-sixty-five year olds (dubbed "the silver generation") generally have large savings and real assets as well as disposable incomes, and despite being brought up to save as much as possible, some of them now seem prepared to spend. They do not seem overly concerned about the drop in house prices, perhaps because they see this as a problem later for their children rather than themselves now.

You should visit the appropriate Chamber of Commerce, as well as your Embassy in Japan, and talk to their people, collect all the information you can, and get a copy of anything of relevance, particularly about the latest movements and fads.

An annual visit helps a lot

If possible, a really senior person from your company should be sent once a year on a short goodwill mission. This will help to develop your relationship and enhance your chances of repeat business. The guy who made the previsit is an ideal choice, as long as he dressed and behaved properly the first time.

Whether or not you send a senior person in advance, it is quite possible that the leader of your team will be invited to meet their go-between or contact person and start the business relationship over drinks and dinner the night before the first meeting. If issued, it is important to accept this invitation. Consider flying in a day or two early if you think you will be too tired or jet-lagged to make a good showing. The person you meet will probably be your conduit to their team for the duration of your visit.

Your local rep should be invited to all meetings

If you can you should keep a local representative in Japan and invite him to all meetings. If you exclude him, it makes him look inferior - the Japanese are likely to think that if you do not bother with him, why should they? If he is not included, after your departure he would find it difficult to work well with them and your interests would therefore suffer. Besides, he really ought to know what is going on.

This local rep. is your go-between and he serves a major purpose in Japan. By separating the two principle leaders involved he can ensure that neither side loses face during negotiations, whether these are early on as both sides sidle towards each other or later on if there is a potential point of conflict. If you try to manage without a go-between you will find it harder to do business, even if you are not aware of the fact.

Five: The Early Meetings

Don't get friendly with the help

When you arrive at a company, it is important not to be too sociable to secretaries and receptionists. In Japan, the female receptionist is low on the totem pole and she will be very embarrassed if you are overly warm and friendly, try to chat to her, or make jokey remarks. She will probably not know what to do and will feel she is losing face which will embarrass her. It will be best for you both if you behave formally, not give more than one small smile of greeting, and definitely do not offer to shake her hand. If you are exuberant with people who are regarded as lowly, it will tarnish your image in the eyes of those you might wish to impress. In Japan, birds of a feather are expected to flock together.

If there is no receptionist you will have to attract the attention of someone working close by. If you can catch an eye, a quick bow from you tends to ensure they feel obliged to help you because you have established a tiny relationship, however minor.

The First Meeting

No business at the first session

This first session is not intended to do any business but is the start of the process of getting to know each other. You often do not need an interpreter at this stage. In fact, if you do not bring an interpreter it actually flatters the Japanese, as it suggests that they are comfortable speaking and hearing English. Remember however to speak slowly and carefully, especially if you have any trace of regional accent, as this increases the chance of those present understanding you. Many Japanese can read English well but have trouble when speaking and listening. For all subsequent meetings you will need an interpreter (see below, pp.88-91).

The mystery of the empty room

When you and your group are shown into the meeting room it may be empty. If this is the case, it is best to stand near the door, so that you can conveniently meet their team as they arrive. Their team leader will be first to enter. Some people choose to stand near the chair at the center of the table facing the door; this is the seat of honor for the chief guest and you will probably be asked to sit there. Do not however sit down until the Japanese arrive, which they will do very shortly, because if you choose to take the seat of honor without being asked, it would appear presumptuous. You will be invited to sit down in the proper place at the appropriate time. Your team will sit on one side, the other team will be seated opposite.

Spotting the leader

It is generally easy immediately to identify the leader of the opposing team. The leader is always male, enters in front of the others, will be introduced to you first, and will be conservatively but immaculately dressed. The others on his team will noticeably defer to him and it will help your position if you try to be just a little deferential towards him also.

Focus on his face and ensure you easily recognize him henceforth. If you are not used to meeting with Asians and recognizing the facial differences, it would be unfortunate if, say, on the second meeting you have forgotten which one he is.

If their leader is given the seat of honor (facing the door and with one's back to the wall) rather than your leader it suggests that he is probably very senior indeed. If you are invited to sit on a couch with the Japanese, their leader will usually sit next to you.

Most often the Japanese team will be entirely male, and you can usually assume that any woman there is likely to be a low level person. This situation is changing but slowly and normally you will be negotiating with men.

Leaders talk to leaders

You must remember to address the leader of their team not one of his underlings. You can sweep their team with the occasional glance, to try to include them in what you say, but the main focus of your attention should always be on the leader. His status, as well as power, demands this. Your manner towards him should be slightly deferential but this need not be overdone. It can be a fine line between being polite and grovelling! If you manage to convince him that you are seriously inferior, which is actually unlikely, he would then tend to become condescending and expect you to defer to him in the negotiations.

There is never any danger of this if you send someone senior as team leader, because they carry status with them. In Japan, respect tends to come with the position rather than the person occupying it.

When you have to address, or listen to, a member of their team who is not the leader, you need not be quite as deferential to him as you were to his leader. In fact, if you were to treat their whole team exactly alike, it might suggest a lack of respect for their leader! Of course you must not be rude or offhand, merely grade the level of deference in your response.

The nuances of status and attitude are finely drawn in Japan, and are clear to all, but it is often difficult for Westerners brought up in a more democratic and egalitarian tradition to understand and get it right. Some foreigners refuse to try. Perhaps they believe that the social and political principles of their own country are simply the best and should be followed when abroad. Others may think that the Japanese should be exposed to these foreign views in order to educate them. Some others perhaps cannot be bothered to think about the issue, or change their ways appropriately. Those who refuse to try fit in to Japanese etiquette tend to find it harder to reach a successful agreement and where they manage to do so, generally take longer. On the other hand they probably feel good about their stance. You have to make your own decision in such matters and establish what your priorities really are: do you want to change the world or do business?

It is a good idea to try to work out the pecking order of their team, remembering that in such a status-conscious society, the precedence in matters of right of entry, being introduced to your team, sitting down or speaking usually runs straight down the line. It is useful to gain some idea of the kind of relative clout that different people might have, particularly if you detect that certain members of their team seem to be more (or less) supportive of your position. Unfortunately, there is no guarantee that their spokesman-leader will actually hold the most power.

The leader who never was

On occasion, the person who appears to be the leader may not actually be so. It has been known for the actual leader to occupy a position on the edge of the group, and say little or nothing, and only reveal his power and status later. This is sometimes a ploy to mislead you; at other times it reflects his lack of confidence in English and he feels that this will be a matter of importance in these particular discussions. It is worth occasionally reminding yourself that real power in Japan rarely goes with high competency in foreign languages. Bearing this in mind, it pays to be polite to all members of their team.

That quiet first meeting

At the first meeting, you might find that the Japanese team is not particularly forthcoming. They may be shy, rather awkward and perhaps uncomfortable. Their command of English may not be all that good and they will be conscious of this. Most Japanese never like risking even a slight danger of losing face in public as they often have a deeply rooted underlying fear of making a mistake or committing a social gaffe. As children, they are taught by their mothers that people will laugh at them if they do not strictly conform. This tends to inhibit them later in life; although they may lose some of this reserve, their behavior will usually remain formal as they try to fit in.

Table 5.1 Your checklist before the first meeting

Am I certain that I have got over jet lag?
Has a senior executive already politely called on his opposite number?
Is it clear who will take notes, type up daily minutes and distribute them?
Am I clear that the initial meeting(s) do not discuss business?
Have I a good Introductory speech for the first proper business meeting?
Have I learned a few polite phrases of Japanese and tried them out?
Have I a lot of business cards on me and are they easily accessible?
Are all team members aware they must not interrupt or use given names?
Am I familiar with what is considered polite in Japan?

What might happen at the first meeting?

The first meeting is designed purely to start to get to know each other and commence the building up of a relationship. This relationship will be expected, on the Japanese side at least, to last for some time. They want to know who they will be dealing with: are you reliable and sincere? Is your company to be trusted? And are you generally civilized? At this stage they are merely sounding you out.

At this first meeting, you can expect the Japanese to enquire politely about your trip, and was it comfortable etc. They may well enquire about the health of colleagues of yours back at HQ that they have met before. If they have previously met, say, two of your colleagues and enquire after one but ignore the other, they might be registering a dislike; take note of this as in future it may pay you to send someone else in the place of the person deliberately slighted in this way. Note that what is *not* said can be important in Japan. Clues and hints about feelings and attitudes abound but they are indirect, and many are missed by foreigners who do not expect such things and do not know what to look for. The Sherlock Holmes story about the importance of the fact that the dog did not bark in the night would make perfect sense in Japan.

You can praise the company being visited and express pleasure at the chance to meet, or to renew the acquaintanceship after a long absence etc., as appropriate. The nonbusiness interest of the Japanese company or its president (which you investigated before you came) can be introduced and praised here.

Although unlikely, if at the first meeting the Japanese company president and a few aides depart, leaving the others with you, it is a signal that some discussion of business is likely to begin. If they do this, the most senior Japanese present will often start by asking about your company or, if you have done business before, recounting the entire history of the dealings between your company and his. You might respond by conveying greetings from your managing director or someone of the equivalent level to the person who just spoke – never from someone lower.

You should try to keep everything very low key and stick to matters of general principle, hopes for cooperation and a long and healthy relationship etc. In particular, this is not the time for specific proposals or any details.

What if their leader suddenly changes?

Should the regular leader disappear for a few days and be replaced by someone younger, expect that something unusual may be in the air. It might be that they are about to concede something important which they do not want to do – and the leader is letting a junior take the blame for not achieving the point they really wanted. On the other hand, it might be that they are about to throw something at you and make a suggestion you will not like, which they feel could cause serious strain on the relationship. In this case their normal leader might prefer to be tactfully absent. As all good politicians are aware, it is a great gift to know when to be out of town. If you observe that the replacement for the original leader is older, better dressed, and with a quiet air of authority, it is often a good sign and may mean they have reached agreement among themselves and are about to conclude and sign. Apart from such changes in the leadership, you should expect changes in the Japanese team as a matter of course and not be disconcerted by them.

Playing the family-name game: alias Smith and Jones

Just as with their team, you should address the members of your own team by their family name not their given name. That is, you should say "Thank you Mr. Smith" not "Thanks, Bill". When referring to them you should also be formal, e.g., "As Mr. Smith said earlier..." This can be hard for Americans or Australians to remember, as it often seems unnatural to them. British visitors perhaps might have less trouble here. The Japanese will use your last names and it gets a bit silly if you keep saying "as John said..." and they reply "But Mr. Jones also suggested..."

The main reason for you sticking to surnames is that the use of first names does not impress. Rather than them feeling that you are a friendly team, all pulling together, they are more likely to decide that you are not businesslike and are unable to separate business and social relationships. The Japanese can keep these quite separate in their minds, even if many apparently social events are really a form of doing business. This is another example of the distinction between surface appearance and underlying reality that is pervasive in Japan. If you really want to impress the other side, you can refer to your own colleague's title – "Thank you Sales Manager Jones".

Good notes mean good records means good business

It is good idea to choose a member of your team to keep clear minutes at every meeting. The Japanese are obsessive about detail and will keep a very accurate and detailed record for their own use, but are unlikely to circulate minutes of meetings to you. You might find that something you raised weeks earlier may suddenly be presented to you as an earlier suggestion of yours that is now accepted – this can work to your disadvantage if you have not kept good records. You might find for example that when you check back on your records, in the context of the earlier meeting the meaning was slightly different from that now being suggested. Or it might have been an idea you made as a kite-flyer to see what their response would be at the time and you did not wish it to be taken seriously, especially without full discussions and these were not held. In any case, if you are familiar with details, it impresses the Japanese.

It is important that you do not take the minutes yourself, as you need to watch the person with whom you are negotiating and listen carefully as to *how* things are said, as well as what is said and to keep an eye open for things that are *not* said. No matter what, powerful people do not take their own notes in hierarchical Japan.

You might find it useful to put the minutes on tape directly after the meeting and get them typed up quickly, so that you can refer to them easily at future meetings. Alternatively, at least one brand of notebook computer has a built in printer and one of your team could compose the minutes directly on the computer and print them out. It is a good idea to photocopy the minutes so that each member of your team can have their own copy.

On Being Introduced

The polite Japanese bow is difficult to do properly

In Japan, a bow without speaking is considered far more polite than actually saying something. It is worth remembering that the smile is not particularly polite in Japan, unlike in most Western countries, but a bow is extremely so. When someone bows to you, it is usually better not to try to reciprocate and bow back. Instead, you should incline your head slowly and carefully, rather like a miniature bow. The reason for avoiding bowing is that it really is not easy for a foreigner to bow properly. It is hard to get the angle right and in any case if you bow, the Japanese will promptly bow back to you – and it is hard to know when to stop! When someone bows to you, you may return a deep and slow head incline. It is impolite not to make some gesture of this kind in return.

Dropping your head in this way when pushing past in front of someone signifies "excuse me", without a word being spoken. It is a good idea to do this and it will be noticed, just as the absence will also be observed critically. You can also give a deep nod of the head, (slowly and deliberately) when meeting someone, apologizing for something, or accepting a present. Patterns of behavior matter in Japan and the totality of how one presents oneself are important. This is what is noticed, not merely the polite words used. You will find that the Japanese often shake hands with foreigners as well as bow. If you feel that you really want to bow, it is not exactly improper but it will not be expected.

The three kinds of bow are all done slowly and carefully

There are three different degrees of bow, each one appropriate to the level of the person opposite and it is important not to use an inappropriate level which looks ludicrous to a Japanese and can easily give offence. The simplest form of bow is to bend at 15 degrees and keep your hands at the side; this is the one to aim for if you feel you must bow. A more respectful bow is at about 30 degrees again with your hands at the side, and you would only do this one with someone of clearly much higher status, e.g. a minister of state. The most respectful sort of bow, *which only Japanese use and you must not*, is at 30 degrees but with the hands placed palm down on the knees.

When bowing, it may be done a few times not just once, the actual number depending on the relationship and circumstances – it is a complex matter involving the occasion, the nature of the relationship and the relative status of those involved, but about three bows is often acceptable.

Note that the bow is never hurried, like a cork bobbing in the sea, but is done in a controlled and measured way.

An unexpected danger in the hand shake – no karate!

When being introduced, do not to thrust out your hand sharply. If the person opposite suddenly bows to you, then you could accidentally hit him on the head! If such a calamity occurs, you should never try to pass it off by attempting to make a joke of it, as might be done in your own culture. You have already made two mistakes, first, getting the bowing business wrong and, secondly, touching the other person's body. Don't make a third mistake and laugh about the incident. Instead, you must apologize formally and sincerely for your clumsiness.

Do not get with the strength

When meeting someone you should avoid using a firm handshake. In the West this is often felt to suggest strength of character and honesty, or perhaps indicate that you are an athletic and fit young executive. This is not so in Japan. The correct handshake is limp, "like a wet fish", and the other person's hand may be barely grasped at all. Some Japanese lightly hold on to the hand longer than you might feel necessary. In Japan, the message given by a typical Western-style strong grip would be aggression and an attempt to bully, revealing you to be uncouth. Your perceived attempt to intimidate would only work to your disadvantage.

Use that business card!

You should always use a business card (*meishi*) when you meet new people. This should be printed in English on one side and Japanese on the other. It is often better to get them printed in Japan, where silly printing errors in Japanese will be avoided and the size will be right. All business cards are exactly the same size in Japan. It is important to have your cards in the standard size for two reasons. The first is that you do not want to immediately stand out as different or peculiar. The second reason is that the Japanese will file your card along with all others in their standard system – you do not wish them to have to trim your large card down to fit the box or, if your card is small, not be able to locate it easily later on. Getting cards printed takes about a day usually.

A well-designed card

You should put any degrees, titles etc., you may have on your business card. Japan is very rank and protocol conscious and letters after the name impress them. If you attended a well-known university, this could usefully appear on your card. Your exact position in the company should be indicated – the Japanese will at once attempt to assess your level and degree of importance and rank you, as they do with each other. Make sure your telephone and fax numbers, including the correct international code, appear on your card. If they have to write to you, they will copy your address exactly as it is on your card, so ensure it is in the proper order and includes the name of your country of residence.

Your cards written in Japanese are only intended for the Japanese

You should never try to use business cards containing Japanese characters when in other Asian countries. This particularly applies to China, Hong Kong, Indonesia, Malaysia or Singapore – i.e., those countries occupied by Japan during the Second World War. The residents there would often be reminded of an unhappy past, feel offended, and probably regard you as both arrogant and ignorant. If your company deals internationally, you should consider getting a unique set of cards for each country you visit, with the national language on the back. This is usually found impressive even to people who speak fluent English. It shows you are trying and they tend to feel warmer at once. Note that cards written in Arabic or in Chinese can be used in several different countries but take care not to use modern Chinese characters if going to Taiwan as they transmit a political message.

Recording information and the business card

You should aim to keep a complete record of everyone you meet, storing their cards safely. Special boxes for storing other peoples' business cards can be purchased in Japan and you should buy one as soon as you can. It is useful to jot down on each card as many personal details as you can as soon as possible after the meeting (see Table 5.2). Remember, however, not to write on anyone's business card in front of them or anyone else, as this would be considered insulting. You must not tear or fold them of course, but this hardly needs saying!

Table 5.2 Some things to write on business cards (but never in front of them!).

Where you met them, the date, and reason for the get-together.
Whether married; the number age and sex of their children.
What their children are doing; which university they attended.
Any sports or hobbies the person prefers.
Any books, films, or TV programs etc. that they may have indicated they enjoyed.
Where they go for their holidays.
Have they been to your country and if so when.
What other foreign countries they have visited and why.
Any distinguishing physical features (to help you recognize them again) and their health if they mentioned it.
Any particular attitudes they express or reveal.
Where he lives and how difficult is his journey home to work.
Any special event or incident that occurred while you were both present.
The general impression they made on you.

The details you note on the card can prove very useful at future meetings or on a subsequent visit to Japan. The information will help to remind you about the individual and you may meet dozens of different people or even hundreds if making the rounds.

On a subsequent day or trip to Japan, if you have met someone before and have forgotten them, they will feel affronted and will probably not be disposed to help you. If however you are able to refer to facts about the particular individual, it demonstrates a personal interest and underlines your sincerity.

You need more business cards than you might imagine

Several hundred will usually be necessary for one visit to Japan, as you must give one to each person when visiting a company or government office and in meetings. At the first meeting, you start by exchanging business cards with each person present. It is best to carry your cards in a special holder in your inside jacket pocket so that you can produce them quickly and easily. Do not carry your cards in your back trouser pocket whether loose or in a wallet and make sure they are clean and not written on, bent or damaged. If you intend to visit several departments or companies, check each day before you set out to make sure you have plenty of perfect cards with you, as it is easy to run out.

The hosts are expected to offer their card first

The senior person present starts and if you remember their sequence, it identifies their pecking order for you. You should offer the card first, preferably holding it in both hands, before shaking hands. The Japanese will often bow as well as shake hands – you as a foreigner should *not* try a full bow but remember that if you incline your head slowly as you shake hands it will be appreciated.

As you receive a card, look at it slowly and carefully

Business cards occupy a more important position in Japan than in the West. You should study carefully each card you are given, and for longer than you would in the West. Never just glance at the business card as you receive it and then put it casually into your pocket, as this would be considered to be most insulting. The card reveals where the person stands in the firm, which in rank and status-conscious Japan matters greatly. In a real way the card symbolizes the person and indeed is almost an extension of the individual. When Japanese exchange *meishi*, they need to scrutinize the other's card to find out the relative level of both people. This has major implications in hierarchical Japan, for the choice of words each will use to speak to the other, as well as the behavior pattern each will adopt.

In Japan, the exchange of cards is also the first step in developing a relationship, and it is not merely telling someone your name or supplying a useful reminder of it later. It is a good idea to incline your head politely as you study the card for a short period of time. If you are meeting a group of Japanese from different institutions or firms, and the person is with a well-known company, it does no harm to murmur out loud the name of the company appreciatively, nod slowly, and try to look impressed.

Other than hosts proffering their business cards first, protocol indicates that younger present to older, while sellers present to buyers. The rule is that the more junior person presents to the more senior. When the host proffers first, he is politely pretending to be the junior as a way of flattering the guest. Note that if you are really well below the level of the person opposite, e.g. you are a CEO of a small company and being presented to a minister of state, or if you are a low level manager meeting the CEO of a large company, it would be regarded as presumptuous for you to offer your card first even though you are the junior. The other person is simply too high up for such a trade to take place. If he offers his card, you are being honored, and should of course immediately offer yours in exchange and hold it in both hands.

Remember to hand over your business card the right way up

It should be facing outward so the recipient can easily read it. In Japan it is considered rude to ignore other peoples' convenience in what often seems to Westerners a small thing (if they notice at all). The same holds true if passing anything to anyone, for example if you offer a book or a stapler, you must turn it so the recipient can use it at once without further manipulation.

Each person gets their own card

You must hand over a business card to each person individually and do it with care. You should never fan them out and offer them like a conjurer, nor deal them out like cards. Nor can you pile them up on the table and ask them to help themselves as some foreigners have tried to do! This would all seem extremely rude and indicate you do not consider the recipient to be worth the slightest effort. It is best not to make any facetious or funny remarks however inconvenient it may seem to be carefully handing out a card at a time to each person. This just might be the death of your hopes for business, even before any negotiations have begun.

English side up?

There are two schools of thought about which side of the card to present to the Japanese. Some feel it is polite to present your card with the English version uppermost which suggests that the other person's linguistic ability is high. The other school of thought says the Japanese side up is better as it makes it easier for them immediately to start the process of working out who you really are and how you stand in relation to them. You should never feel that presenting the side of the card in Japanese will impress by demonstrating that you have bothered to put their language on the card. They expect that you will automatically take care of such essential courteous details anyway.

On the whole, the Japanese side uppermost is probably your best bet; not everyone can be guaranteed to notice the implied "He's good at English" compliment but all those inconvenienced by the foreign language will definitely know it.

You and your company

As you introduce yourself, it is common to state the company you work for. Many Japanese will mention their company name before their own. Identification with and loyalty to the company is strong in Japan and a person is seen as a group member of a particular company rather than as a lone individual. There is a strong need to belong. You are expected to be proud of your company; putting your name and company in one breath demonstrates this, as well as categorizing you. As part of this identification of company and self, you should never criticize your own company or any past decisions it may have made. Equally, you should not criticize their company in any way, as it will be taken as a personal insult. If there is a problem between you, then you can and should engage in self-criticism. For example, you could perhaps blame your own inadequacy at not having seen earlier that they might take the words to mean X when you felt it meant Y. That is far more acceptable than saying "We interpret the agreement to mean Y", or something which directly explains your position. The meaning of both approaches is identical, but the form in which it is expressed can make life easy or difficult for you.

Laying down your cards

You may put the cards you receive on the table in front of you. This is not considered at all rude, but rather a sensible thing to do. You will find it useful to lay them out in the order that people are seated, so that you can check on who is speaking to you, learn their names, and not get confused. A person will not be offended if when he starts to speak (it will rarely be a she, even if any women are present) you glance at his business card. If after some time you notice the team opposite beginning to pick up your team's business cards, it is a sign that the meeting is concluding. There is a protocol even here: if you are dealing with a person senior to you, he puts away your card before you put away his! Similarly, buyers put away before those hoping to sell.

When you leave the room, remember to pick up all their business cards carefully and take them away. If you accidentally left one behind, the person would be deeply offended and would lose face before the others. The cards should be placed in your special case for carrying them and not placed in your wallet, and *especially* not in your back pocket.

Generalities of Meetings

You can expect to be served a drink by an Office Lady

The OL will probably serve you green tea without milk or sugar. Whatever you are given, accept it without being effusive. Do not start to drink this until invited to do so and then sip it slowly and gracefully. Even if you are thirsty, try not to upend the cup and drink it down in a gulp, which is considered grossly impolite and greedy. Other drinks may be served later.

Japanese teams work as a unit

They usually organize beforehand and discuss everything, reaching agreement on what it is hoped to get, what arguments will be presented, how this can best be done, and maybe what the fall-back position could be. It is not exactly democratic in these private discussions: the consensus arrived at is likely to be one that has been heavily influenced by suggestions and hints from the most powerful person present, who will guide and structure the discussion to the final decision. It is rare for him to issue orders as they are not necessary; the wishes and suggestions of the superior party are quickly grasped and followed by the inferior.

Once negotiating with you, who will say what is not normally an issue: the leader will speak for all. They will present a united front and not engage in argument among themselves in front of you. This will not prevent them from lapsing briefly into Japanese now and then in your presence to discuss a point. It helps them immensely that few Westerners speak Japanese so that they can openly converse in the same room; your team does not get the same advantage because some of them will definitely understand English.

Polite formulas rule

You should not show surprise at the polite formulae that take up the start of any meeting. Expect this to happen, it always does. Do not show either incredulity or boredom, just keep looking interested and be polite, make small-talk, and wait for the other side to introduce any business. You are already negotiating! In Japan, it is normal to start a conversation by referring to common friends so do not be surprised if your opposite number does this. You are advised do this yourself, as it will help to make them feel relaxed and comfortable.

Your small-talk beginning

You should have ready a few topics to serve as ice breakers before business can begin. You can often start by mentioning the weather; if possible this should be done in a way that shows concern for the other party, e.g., saying "It is awfully warm and humid today, isn't it?" in a sympathetic tone. Do not, however, add a phrase like "in here"; this would be taken as a criticism and probably as an indirect or implicit request to turn up the air-conditioning! If you actually feel it is too hot or too cold and would like the temperature altered, this indirect way is the best one to adopt. Similarly, it is best not to use a phrase that criticizes Tokyo or Japan. In hot weather, asking about the other party's health in view of the heat is considered to be polite and you could try that.

It is always safe to enquire whether the other party has been affected by any external events such as heavy rain or a serious earthquake and how they are coping with it. Other than the weather, a local newspaper will usually provide a few topics of contemporary interest, such as a visiting art exhibition, to which you can refer.

Your first speech is as important as a baby's first word

It is wise to spend a lot of time preparing a careful introductory speech; you will deliver this at your first genuine business meeting. You do not need one for the high-level social call or the introductory small-talk session. However, you might choose to have your important opening address prepared well ahead of time and carry it with you, just in case they decide to turn what you felt was a small-talk meeting into a genuine business one. It is usually a good idea to stick to your prepared script – reading it out verbatim is desirable.

The importance of this introduction cannot be overstressed as it lays the groundwork for the entire future. You can discuss the history of your company, what you produce or sell, where your main markets are, how you see Japan fitting in to your company's future, where you hope to go together, and so on. The reason for scripting the introduction carefully is that whatever is said now goes on the record and can be referred to later. This is about your only chance to get in a word about general philosophy, unless the negotiations flounder and you then chose to deliberately hold a "Let's look over the history of the relationship" session. Should this happen, if whatever is holding up the negotiations and proving to be a sticking point was covered in general terms in your introduction, you are in a good position to point this out, and demonstrate that what you want is well within the spirit of the negotiations so far, or alternatively what they are suggesting might fall outside the earlier agreed approach and principles.

No details in your opening speech

You should keep all details out of this first speech. Right now you are establishing general principles and a framework within which all future meetings and discussions will be held. It is often a good idea to mention how this particular bit of business fits in with your company's long term goals and expectations in the broad sense. This would give a desirable feeling of a continuing long term presence and planning to your proposal.

You must especially avoid details like product specifications, construction material, prices, sizes, or delivery dates. Such matters are inappropriate for early meetings and should be reserved for later. You might try to let the Japanese be the first to move to details, as they will always choose a time with which they are comfortable. If you try to start too early, it might actually hold things up as they might then have to hold meetings without you to consider what to do to deal with this unwanted and unexpected move of yours.

Principles before details

The general approach of always trying to introduce and discuss your long term generalized goals before turning to specifics should be followed. What you lay down as broad principle helps to shape the meetings to come. In Japan, all negotiations normally move from the general to the particular; first the framework is set and later the details will later be thrashed out within its confines.

Although the approach of putting principles before details is standard in Japan, on rare occasions the Japanese have been known to reverse it! Some negotiators have had the experience of the Japanese team jumping straight into discussing the details and seemingly uninterested in discussing generalities. Why did they do this? It may be shock tactics on their part (as they feel are taking a surprising and shock approach) and they are trying to unsettle you. A simpler explanation is that they may merely be trying to adopt Western negotiating patterns and using an approach that they think will be acceptable to you and keep you happy.

This is the more likely explanation, particularly if you are dealing with a major company which has experienced people who are well versed in the ways of foreigners. Of course, you might not even notice that they have cut out the stage of generalities, since in Western eyes they are not behaving abnormally.

"What a good meeting we had!"

It is always valuable to mention any earlier meeting favorably. It is in fact thought rude not to do so and if you forget to this, it might be taken as a silent criticism of past events. You will recall that what is not said carries a message to any sensitive Japanese, just as space in a painting or between rocks in a garden is meaningful. Starting with some polite words about the last joint meeting you held is often your best way into the meeting. Something along the lines of "We had an interesting and fruitful discussion yesterday", "It was such a pleasant visit to the temple", or "We all had a most enjoyable time at the restaurant last night", depending on what you had actually done, would make the opposition feel good and help to make you look civilized in their eyes.

Patience definitely is a virtue

The first rule of dealing with the Japanese is to be patient, go slow, and not to rush things. The gradual build up means you have the time to gain the confidence of the other team. Things take time to achieve in Japan. You should aim to build up your relationship slowly, maintain a low-key approach, and not to be "hail-fellow-well-met" at the initial meeting. Friendship and a good relationship are not instantly acquired; a warm, openhearted and demonstrative approach that would appear friendly, in say Texas, comes across as shallow, insincere, vulgar and brash in Japan. To a business person or public servant, a new contact is almost frighteningly unknown and such a person will not automatically be accepted as reliable; it takes time to gain their confidence. It can be five or six years before the business relationship seems sound from the Japanese end.

When you start to address a meeting, ease into what you want to do!

It is most important *not* to jump in at once and start to present your case. If you do this, you will puzzle and perhaps alienate those present. Even when you have already held several meetings and this particular one has been specifically set up for you to make a presentation, you should still not start to do so immediately. It is better to begin with a reference to the last meeting, with a statement about how useful it was, perhaps followed by a recapitulation of the main goals and intentions of both sides, and a brief history what has been agreed so far. This allows you to ease into your presentation and everyone will feel comfortable with you. A bald "Well, let's go, this is what I have put together" approach is not appreciated and will almost certainly be counterproductive.

It is best to hide your deadlines

You should try to avoid committing yourself to a deadline for leaving. It is crucial not to say immediately you arrive that you will negotiate "until the 17th then fly back home or go on to country X". Always try to leave your departure date open and imply that you are prepared to stay and negotiate indefinitely. There have been cases in the past where the Japanese knew the departure date, and stalled the foreigners until just before their time to leave, when they were suddenly presented with a take-it-or-leave-it proposition. You can seriously weaken your negotiating position if your departure date is known in advance.

The sweet sound of harmony

You have a permanent need to keep harmony in negotiations, however difficult. This does not mean agreeing to anything that they want, but it does mean avoiding blunt refusals. It is far better to say you will have to consult with others first, or say you will think it over carefully, rather than to say "no". A blunt "no" is felt to involve the opposite party in a loss of face, so that if you say it, it will offend them, and you naturally wish avoid this. It is important always to strive to maintain contact and avoid any confrontations, even if you find something really irritating or unacceptable.

Language and Interpreters

Negotiating in your own language is best

During the negotiations, you should always speak in English, assuming that is your language, and go though an interpreter. You should not speak in Japanese, unless you are totally fluent and have enough experience to understand the sophisticated nuances of the language and culture. For a foreigner speaking Japanese, it is incredibly easy to insult someone owing to the rigid ranking system, the complex set of relationships, and the need to use or avoid certain proper words that must only be used on specific occasions. For instance, different words or phrases must be used when addressing someone who is more important, less important or of the same degree of importance. Getting this wrong can be a dreadful insult; their emotional response dictates that they will feel unsettled or unhappy, even if intellectually they understand that as a foreigner you have simply made an easy mistake.

You should however learn enough Japanese to say hello and get around. Increasingly, Japanese business people and officials expect you to demonstrate some familiarity with the language, however little. A few words of Japanese strengthen your seriousness in their eyes and can lead to a more rapid build up of the relationship.

Simple short sentences satisfy

When negotiating, you should use simple language and short sentences. This is partly because it is always easier for nonnatural English speakers if you do; but a further reason is that in Japanese, unlike in English, the verb goes at the end of the sentence which means the interpreter usually has to hear the whole sentence before he or she can really start to translate. A long sentence can throw the interpreter off balance and lead to mistranslation or inadvertently missing out part of what you said in English.

You must of course avoid double negatives, as they are simply confusing to foreign listeners. "Not that I am saying it is not a good idea, but don't you think we should perhaps avoid a commitment at this stage?" can be difficult to understand let alone render into a foreign language, and you would probably receive blank looks.

Please don't let me be misunderstood

If people do not understand something, they will not tell you. It is not possible for them to interrupt you for two reasons: first, an interruption would be terribly rude in itself and, second, it would be too difficult for them to contemplate, as admitting a lack of understanding would cause a serious loss of face. This means that everyone will look as if they are following, whatever happens. The result is that you will not know that a mistranslation has occurred or appreciate that everyone present may in fact be floundering. Much time can be wasted if you continue to talk, believing that you are having a discussion, but in fact the other side is no longer with you.

What you can do to get around the problem is to repeat the same point in several different ways which often helps to get your meaning across. This is actually liked rather than being resented. Only if you are clearly dealing with people who speak totally fluent English and perhaps they have asked you to speak in this language could it be a mistake to repeat your meaning in this way. Naturally, it would be in your interest to reduce the possibility of misunderstandings developing by speaking clearly and slowly, and avoiding slang and colloquialisms.

You need that interpreter

You should always use an interpreter for the actual negotiations. If you speak any Japanese, it is best to keep it for socializing, although a little Japanese during your introductory speech would go down well. To get the best out of your negotiations, you need your own interpreter, not one supplied by their company. You should carefully brief your interpreter beforehand on any technical phrases that you might wish to use, as well as indicate what sort of broad things you will wish to discuss, and the approach you intend to adopt. Showing the interpreter the proposed agenda often helps, but be aware that the Japanese often deviate from set agendas, so that you cannot rely on that method alone. It is best not to use a Korean as your interpreter, even if born in Japan and therefore totally fluent. The Japanese team would not be impressed by your choice or judgment.

An exception to the rule that you should negotiate in English through interpreters is when the Japanese team really is totally fluent in English and they ask to negotiate in that language. Under such circumstances it would of course be rude to insist upon using interpreters. If they lapse into Japanese to discuss a point, you must accept that you will not know what they are saying, without your own interpreter present.

The big number problem

When referring to a large number, say anything over a hundred thousand, it is desirable to write it down, or check to see that the interpreter does this. The Japanese, like the Chinese, count in units of tens, hundreds, and thousands, but do not go to millions; instead they move to units of ten thousands and then on to one hundred million. A million then has to be translated as "one hundred ten-thousands" and it is surprisingly easy to get the translation wrong by a factor of ten.

The dangers of negotiating in English without an interpreter

- They are unlikely to tell you if they do not understand something, so you can easily think they know more about what you want and are offering than they really do.

- Each side may understand the same word in a different way (e.g. "negotiations" – see Chapter 6, p.102).

- The team opposite may not be able to explain something to you which is of major importance.

- It is difficult for a Japanese to say "no" in his own language and it is even harder for him to work out how to do it in a foreign one.

- Many Japanese are acutely conscious of not speaking English well and they tend to concentrate on not making mistakes which can cause them to miss important points of substance.

Keeping the same interpreter

If possible, try to use the same interpreter for the whole series of meetings. In this way, he or she will become familiar with the particular vocabulary needed, as well as your delivery speed and style of expression. The interpreter will also be aware of the background to the current session, which can prove extremely useful. If you are using one interpreter, rather than a team, you might find that taking a ten-minute break every hour or so will get you better results, as translating can be tiring work and you do not want the quality to suffer.

You may have to dig in your heels

If the Japanese object to you using your own professional interpreter you should insist. You must of course do this in a quiet, authoritative, and non-bullying manner. If they do this, they are probably trying to gain an advantage over you, thinking you will be forced to use their interpreter. It might also mean that some of their team are fully fluent in English and possess experience of working abroad which has given them the ability to read your body language and assess what you are up to. Without your own interpreter you would be denied the opportunity to evaluate theirs.

Six: Subsequent Negotiations–Your Approach

What to Do

Prepare your material in advance

When you have a lot of specific information such as complex data to communicate it is a good idea to present it in previously prepared form. This might be a set of overhead transparencies of raw data but it would be better organized into graphs, bar charts, flowcharts, or pie-diagrams. You should use any visual aids that you think will help explain your product or proposal. These are well-liked by Japanese listeners and you ensure that the communication of your message is clearer. It is worth spending time thinking about what questions you might be asked and getting someone to gather the data you need for a precise answer and also organizing the data in a variety of different ways. If you have the material in your briefcase and do not need it, there is no harm done; but when you do need it, you've got it.

It would be valuable to have plenty of photocopies of your presentation items to give out; remember the Japanese fascination with information and data and always try to include plenty of figures and hard facts. It is useful for both sides if you hand over a copy of all your prepared speeches.

Most Japanese business people take a longer view than occidentals – you might think in terms of the current year plus perhaps the subsequent three or four years. However, ten years is not too long for the people with whom you will be dealing and this extended view could be reflected in your documentation. Perhaps a section like "where we might be a decade from now" could be included for instance - whatever works best for you.

It is most probable that the members of their team read English a good deal better than they speak it, and they will be comfortable knowing that they can look up in the documentation something you say that they feel a bit unsure about. They save face doing this quietly later and will almost certainly be unwilling to ask questions that reveal their (as they feel it) inadequacy. Incidentally, you are better off handing over your documents in English rather than in the form of a poor translation into Japanese: they will understand the former but might easily feel let down or even insulted by the latter.

Look before you leap!

It is wise not to speak until you are asked to do so. The Japanese preference for doing many things in a set and established way, not making it up as they go along, applies also to meetings. There is a prescribed order that the meeting will follow, despite the possible lack of an agenda, and you will get your turn. In Japan, listening without interruption is seen as a sign of authority; interrupting is thought of as rude and a bit childish.

The Japanese generally do not like to forward their opinion until they are asked and are uncomfortable with the idea of people pooling views, debating them, and interrupting each other in open argument. During private group discussions among themselves it is common to go round asking each in turn what they think, and all listen courteously to the views expressed.

"My government, right or wrong"

Always support your own government and do not offer criticisms of it. If you point to imperfections in your country, it would shock the Japanese and you should try to avoid showing even mild disrespect. The Japanese are intensely nationalistic as well as used to living in a structured society. What the government does or says is beyond reproach and even minor criticisms carry a strong feeling of *lesé-majesté*. The most you can say about your own government's failings is to admit that sometimes there are problems and delays, or the behavior of public servants cannot always be predicted accurately.

Making changes later can be difficult

Try to get things right the first time. You are likely to find it difficult if along the track you wish to change something that has been previously agreed. If you ask for a change, and the Japanese dig in their heels and refuse to consider it, the problem may well be the *nemawashi* system of having to get a consensus from many other departments. The people with whom you are dealing will already have secured the agreement of others for the main points and any change suggested by you might mean that they have to go back and start over. The last time they probably had to argue to overcome opposition from some groups, so that those with whom you are negotiating will often be reluctant to restart the process. They might also lose face if it looks, or could be made to look by any opponents within their firm, as if they are going back because they have failed or lost in some way. It is important to do your homework, lay out the general line at the first proper business meeting, and not to try to wing it later as you go. If you make your first business omelette with insufficient thought it is always going to be an impossible task to unscramble it later.

If you really feel that you have to ask for a change

If things go wrong, you might need to ask for some minor change, such as rescheduling a meeting or a revised delivery date. The way you ask for changes matters, so you should do it with great care. You must not blame others for delay, or criticize any earlier agreement you reached about timing. It would be acceptable to say "It is taking longer than I thought" or "I do not work quickly enough" etc., which contain a desirable element of self criticism. You can use a phrase such as "As you will be well aware..." if explaining that things are going wrong. When asking for a change, you should use apologetic phrases like "I strongly regret the inconvenience" or "I hesitate to put you to so much trouble". A soft approach along these lines will often smooth over the event and allow you to get what you want without giving offence. A small bow accompanying an apology or request for understanding when a problem has arisen strengthens the request dramatically.

Profit can be a dirty word

The deep concern for human relations and harmony mean that you might find it useful not to mention profitability but instead to lay stress on other positive sides of the proposal. If you suggest that it can lay the foundation for a long term relationship or strengthen the existing one, it always helps. More concrete things such as market share (without mentioning rivals) and growth in output are valuable points to make. It is also important to stress any possible benefits for the customers of the firm and the company employees themselves, which usefully focuses on group feeling and loyalty. If you can make a case that the Japanese government would benefit in some way, even better. You can then let profitability emerge later almost as an additional benefit. Tacking on "Of course, neither of us would lose from it" makes the profitability point without promoting the idea that you are a cold calculating profit maximizer. Such people may be felt uncivilized and are easily disliked.

You might also find that a suggestion that you could both save money by doing something is a better approach than baldly stating both you and they could make more profit by doing it. Such an indirect approach is readily understood and liked.

Surprises win no prizes

It is best to send a draft well in advance – say at least five weeks. If you spring a draft contract on anyone or produce one at a meeting without warning, it merely adds to the delay. The Japanese need time to explore the contents themselves and then discuss it with all the relevant departments and ministries that might be involved. If you do suddenly appear with a document, you are likely to find that the negotiations suddenly cease, until the discussions with others involved are complete – this can cost you both time and money.

Setting your price

When you finally get around to discussing price, you should expect the Japanese to bargain hard. You naturally have to build some leeway into your first offer, as in all bargaining processes. You should try not to make it unreasonably high (if selling), however, as the Japanese will have investigated the market carefully and be well aware of the going rates and prices. They are likely to distrust you if your initial offer is well out of line with the market. You will find if valuable if you can explain why you are asking a little more than the market price, for example, you offer special services, faster delivery, brochures in Japanese, or good after-sales follow up etc., whatever seems appropriate to your case. You or your personal assistant could usefully spend time before going to Japan inventing a list of possible justifications for the price you hope to get or pay. You might be grateful for having put in the effort if you are suddenly asked to justify your price.

Keep some concessions for later

Try not to make too many concessions in the early stages. The typical Western approach to negotiating is to go through points in order, using an agenda, and settle them one by one, like jumping a series of hurdles in a race. When there are no more points left, the negotiations are considered over, agreement has been reached, and the contract etc., is signed. In Japan it is quite different. They adopt a more holistic approach, with wide-ranging discussions going backwards and forwards over many of the points. This means you will often find yourself reconsidering a point which you thought had already been settled. The Japanese approach is really a reflection of their philosophy of life, which is seen as an interconnected stream of ongoing elements. From a practical viewpoint, it means that if you make concessions as you go, in your accustomed way, you will have little left to give up in exchange at the end when many of the details may suddenly be decided.

You should be aware that it is customary in Japan to throw in a little something as a concession or sweetener after the conclusion of the agreement. This means it is desirable for you to keep something up your sleeve, just in case, which you can then politely offer at the proper time.

The meeting without a decision

You will find that in many meetings there will be no clear decision reached about anything. Few decisions in Japan are ever made in a direct meeting between the two sides. The *nemawashi* (consultation) and *ringi* (signed off piece of paper) system means that often no decision can be reached even if you make a suggestion which is liked by all present. The leader opposite, who may strongly agree with you and wish to accept, is unable to commit others who are absent. You have to accept this is the situation and try not to fret at delays.

Behind the scenes and unknown to you, intense discussions may be going on. You might find that for a long period of time nothing much seems to happen and then things suddenly resolve when you have perhaps begun to lose hope.

Say it again, Sam

Whilst negotiating, you should not be afraid to repeat a point if you think there might have been the slightest misunderstanding or if someone left the room earlier and has now returned. In Japan, people tend to wander in and out during negotiations, especially later in the process, when they feel comfortable with you. Some important people might have left the room at a crucial time and missed something that they really need to know. If you are seen as taking care of everyone and ensuring harmony it will help your cause not harm it. It is easy to become bored and start to feel irritated when they keep going back to something you thought had already been discussed to death, but conceal it if you do.

If they keep returning to a point, it may be that they are testing your position carefully and are not fully convinced about you and your company. Yet it may simply be that they feel that going over the issues in this way strengthens group-feeling – most people are happy with repetitions.

You can expect to have to keep going over the same issue if new people are brought in. These may be there because you are forcing them into an area where they might have to make unexpected concessions and the new men are to monitor and judge.

It could also be that a different government department has suddenly got interested in the negotiations, and these are bureaucrats who wish to deal with you directly, rather than go through the *nemawashi* process of behind-the-scenes agreement. Whatever the reasons, you must hide any irritation you feel at going over the matter yet again, speak slowly, and avoid any tendency to raise your voice which could reveal your displeasure.

When they ask the impossible

If the other team proposes something that you cannot accept, you have to find a way of rejecting it but without disagreeing strongly and openly. You do this by registering your protest softly and gently, perhaps by opening with a phrase such as "I am probably wrong here...", "I am no expert but...", "I could easily be mistaken however..." or at its strongest "As we see it..." The idea is to adopt a self-critical approach and then make your point – you can say just about anything (softly and quietly, avoiding insults) once you have first gone through a polite disclaimer.

The power of a humble apology

If there is a problem on your side, then what we think of as a humble apology is required. This might run along the lines of your failure to understand the issue correctly or not to have acted in a timely or proper manner. Note the element of self-criticism, which is essential to achieve the correct degree of regret. Such an approach can be surprisingly effective at restoring harmony and can even get a faltering relationship back on track. An expensive gift, professionally wrapped and delivered after your apology, will strengthen the newfound harmony.

Be wary if you suddenly receive a gift

In Japan, gifts can be given for a variety of reasons and if you unexpectedly receive one it is a good idea to ask one or two Japanese colleagues or friends why they think you got it and what it might indicate. If you do not do this, the giver may wonder why you did not respond correctly (if a response is indicated and expected). Possibly worse, you may find that accepting the gift means that at some time in the future you will have to repay the favor, perhaps in a way you do not like (see Gift Giving, pp.136-41).

Pushing for a critical delivery date can backfire

You should not take promised delivery dates too seriously, even if written into the contract, as they might not be met. If you push strongly for a particular date and they see that you feel it is important, they may agree to your date simply in order to please you and to maintain harmony. They might do this even though they know perfectly well that the date cannot possibly be met, but they consider that is preferable to engaging in a slugging match on such a minor issue. When the delivery fails to appear, you can expect an apology but that will probably not help you much. When you are negotiating, it is often better to accept a date that they think is reasonable rather than to persist in arguing for a date they will perhaps renege on later.

Tell me why? Asking for an explanation can be tricky

If you do not understand something, be careful how you ask for an explanation. To many Japanese it would be seen as a crass piece of behavior if you say "Could you repeat that please?", although this would be a normal Western thing to do. The Japanese are much less direct. The best way to do it and keep harmony is first to hesitate a moment, then apologize for not understanding the issue etc. or failing to pay proper attention, and finally go on to ask them what you missed. Self-deprecation will take you further and quicker even if you find it hard to do at first. Believe me, after the first few times it gets easier!

When you think you have an agreement, stop and check

You need to be very careful when you think you have reached an agreement because what you actually have may be an understanding that they will consider your proposal, rather than an agreement itself. This confusion has regularly happened in the past.

It is desirable that towards the end of each meeting you go over what was discussed and spell out what has been agreed, so that both sides know where they stand and are in accord.

During the negotiating process, if both sides agree that a contract will follow, it is useful to try to get an agreement on the date for the actual signing of the contract, as this can hasten the consensus-seeking and speed up the *ringi* system. But do not tell them you will be forced to leave at that time.

It is worth noting that if there are only one or two people present at the meetings you may eventually have no deal, even if negotiations appear to be continuing. In Japan, it needs a lot of people to get an agreement, but it takes only one to refuse.

Your Japanese agent can make or break you

The man you select as your local representative should have gone to the right university, have many contacts, and enjoy wide esteem. If you do not manage to find such a person, you are wasting your time and money. In Japan, contacts made at school and university are scrupulously maintained throughout an entire business life and new contacts are steadily added. The Japanese business systems revolve around contacts, friendship, long term relationships, and mutual trust. Japanese business is like a huge old-boys network and that is what you are trying to buy into with your local representative. If your representative is not totally suitable and lacks access to the proper high levels, you might find that you have inadvertently joined the lower school and are not allowed to play with the big boys.

Time spent choosing your Japanese representative is never time wasted.

Suggestions are made to equals

In the informal part of doing business, when drinking with their team or out for dinner, if you wish to make a serious suggestion, make sure that you do so to your ranking opposite number. Remembering their hierarchical approach, you need to raise issues on the basis of equality, and not with some junior member of their team. Bear in mind that such an idea floated under such circumstances does not carry commitment, and is often kite flying. Try to watch for such indirect approaches from their side as well as making your own.

Rest is your secret weapon

As part of your tactics, you should ensure that you get plenty of rest. Japanese "salarymen" are used to going out drinking and socializing several times a week and regard it as part of their job. They are really tough! Some of them might be younger and with more stamina than your team because you are deliberately sending revered older people. In addition, your team has to be present at all meetings whereas they can choose to rotate people to keep them fresh and alert. It is difficult for many Western business people to stay up until gone eleven o'clock each night, pouring down alcohol and singing in karaoke bars, then feel at their best and ready to negotiate the following morning.

With this in mind, if you notice that they regularly switch team members, you might start to suspect that they are trying to wear you down by sitting in relays to allow some of them to rest. They will normally be less tired in any case, because they have a large team with all the backup they need, while you probably have only a small team without backup, and cannot prepare as well. They are not suffering from culture shock either which you may be even if you do not recognize the fact. Make sure you get enough evenings off and explain politely that you have work to do which they will understand and cannot object to – then go to bed early instead!

If problems build up

If you feel that negotiations are going nowhere and suspect there may be hidden problems, a tactic worth trying is to arrange a special meeting of both sides specifically to look over the entire history of the relationship between the two companies, or if you are a government negotiator, the two countries.

You should plan your speech most carefully, going back to basics and generalities, including your long-term hopes. Then you can go over the history of the present negotiations carefully, examining the issues involved, and how each side has tackled them so far. If you make a few rather humble remarks about your own poor ability as a negotiator and where you might possibly have made mistakes, it will impress the Japanese and there is a good chance that the other team will respond well and eventually indicate where the problem, if any, lies. Hopefully they will also start to see your team as civilized and trying hard in the proper way – as a result they should start to relax and be more understanding. From this changed atmosphere, a fruitful discussion of problems and possible solutions might emerge.

What Not to Do

Try not to become annoyed if your appointment is not kept

This can be irritating when you went to a lot of trouble to set it up in the first place. Many Japanese, like South Americans, have a rather different attitude to time than, say North Americans and Northern Europeans. The Japanese are more people-oriented and prefer to build networks and relate to the people they are with, rather than to stick to some rigid timetable set in advance. If meeting with others and things start to run late, they may well decide to continue and not break off to keep their appointment with you. The price of having to put off some other individual down the track is often felt worth paying to retain harmony and friendship.

When dealing with foreigners, they really do try to make agendas, stick to timetables, and keep to appointment schedules. In large part they do this because they know that this is important to the foreign guests and they are trying to alter their normal business habits to please you. When dealing among themselves, however, they are much less rigid and considerably less punctilious about things like time. They will spend much effort trying to reach a consensus within the group, or going through polite formulae at meetings, even when it means overrunning the programed time.

As a result, they might be late for a subsequent meeting or miss an appointment entirely and have to reschedule it. In America or Northern European, to keep someone waiting may be a power play used to indicate relative status or gain an edge in the bargaining to come. In Japan, if one of your appointments is cancelled or you are kept waiting you should not automatically feel it is a deliberate ploy. More probably, the people you wish to see are not able to leave the group session in which they are involved in and are merely victims of the system. In many cases they will simply not be aware that you will have a problem with this, as in their world such an action is normal and not considered rude. Try to restrain any feelings of anger – and if you do feel any, do not let them show.

"Negotiation" can be a grubby word

In English the word "negotiation" has a feeling of equality and holding discussions in order to reach a mutually acceptable and beneficial conclusion. In sharp contrast, the word in Japanese carries a feeling of anger, fighting, or confrontation. Bargaining with anyone tends to seem a little crude and vulgar to many Japanese; it is not unlike the Nineteenth Century upper-class English attitude towards "trade", which was despised as being beneath one's dignity. Some Japanese find it a little difficult to engage in "negotiation", because of the feeling of dispute between the two parties that the word carries. It sharply conflicts with their desired approach of seeking consensus. You are advised not to mention that you are engaged in negotiations with them, and certainly not to keep stressing it, just in case it upsets the Japanese team or even antagonizes the more traditional among them. If you must refer to the negotiations it is better to use an indirect phrase, like "the chance to exchange views", "the discussions we are having" or simply say "the talks".

If you listen in silence it will worry them – so don't!

When listening, you should nod your head or say something in agreement. You should say something like "yes", "fine", or "I see" if the Japanese negotiator pauses while speaking. The Japanese get uncomfortable when they speak into a void; the person listening is supposed to keep reassuring them that they are paying attention and are involved in the relationship. As a consequence, they say "*hai*" (yes) constantly while someone else is talking to them, either directly or when on the telephone. This "yes" does not signify agreement, or mean anything very much really. If you nod, or say "Mmh", "yes", "indeed" or "really", it encourages them to proceed and tends to make them feel more kindly disposed towards you.

Don't lay your metaphysical cards on the table

Indirectness is valued in Japan. This means you should proceed slowly, avoid bluntness, and sidle up to issues in a cautious way. Laying your cards on the table is not seen as a virtue in Japan and there is virtually a taboo on it. We tend to be frank and straightforward in the West, at least by the standards of the culture in Japan and in most Middle-Eastern countries. When in the West we need an answer to a question, usually we simply ask it. This is rather unnerving for a Japanese person, who would prefer you to raise the general area of interest first, then perhaps mention the international situation and how it affects these issues, before going on to indicate some of your views, and then finally get around to posing the actual question.

In Japan, negotiators commonly give hints about what they are seeking as an indication of where they wish to go rather than telling you outright. If you listen carefully to what they say, you will probably find that the Japanese get some of their questions answered without actually asking them at all! Perhaps as a result of this indirect approach, some people believe that the Japanese are essentially a secretive people, who try to conceal what they are about. Really, it is just the culture.

Try to avoid asking negative questions

In Japanese, the grammar is specific – if you ask "You don't want tea do you?" you are likely to get a "yes", (I don't want tea) response, which you may interpret as the person wanting tea. The appearance of tea would then baffle the Japanese who had clearly indicated a preference. In any case, with the question posed in this negative way, the person who will look in the usual Japanese fashion for nuances and hidden meanings will probably feel that you do not want him or her to drink tea and as a result is likely to refuse politely, even when the person really would have liked the tea! In this case, the drink might well have helped the negotiations to proceed better but a lack of communication has got in the way.

The difficulties with "no"

Most Japanese find it hard to say "no" openly and you should avoid it also. You will find that ambiguity during discussions is common and indeed seems almost to be prized; you must accept this and should try not to become irritated by imprecision. In traditional society, which consisted of the classes of samurai, farmer, artisan and merchant, a samurai was allowed to chop off the head of a member of any other class in the community without being punished or being taken to court. Under such circumstances, a straight "yes" or "no", delivered incautiously, could literally prove fatal. It was generally safer to proffer an ambiguous answer, which could be open to interpretation. This habit, prompted by survival instincts, may have influenced society to value uncertain or vague answers.

There are other reasons for many Japanese preferring indefinite or obscure responses. In Japan, saying "no" is felt to offend and might cause some loss of face to the recipient. A desire to avoid placing you in such an embarrassing situation encourages ambiguous answers. Furthermore, if a definite response is given and it later turns out to have been incorrect or not supported by his or her group, that person then loses face. Yet another factor that precludes a straight "yes" or "no" is that it is usually not possible for a single person to commit the company to anything, as whenever something new is proposed, the person will have to go off and obtain agreement from others.

Adding to the ambiguity, the Japanese also tend on occasions not to finish sentences, leaving the other party to finish it in their own mind and sense the meaning. Things are often not laid out in an obvious way, but hidden meanings are built in by one side to be discovered by the other. Negotiations can sometimes seem frustrating when you cannot discover if they agree or disagree with what you suggest. With all the pressure to avoid open commitment, it sometimes seems surprising that agreement is ever reached at all!

Try not to use the word "no" yourself but find a suitable and roundabout way of refusing things (see Table 6.1, p.105). If you disagree with some proposition, it is often a good idea to start by agreeing and say something like "that's right, but..." or "that is a good idea, however..." to indicate your disagreement.

The indirect phrases that often mean "no"

You need to watch for the hidden refusals. For the uninitiated, they can sometimes be difficult to notice and decode. Phrases like "I will do my best" often mean no (see Table 6.1, p.105).

You should listen carefully for such oblique phrases. If they look at each other before replying and then come up with a vague statement, it almost certainly means a refusal. If you get a silence rather than a reply, you can assume that it means no.

Table 6.1 Some phrases that usually mean "no" in Japan

I will do my best.
Let me think about it.
Leave it with me.
I will see what can be done.
I am not sure.
I cannot say at this time.
It's a bit difficult.
I will certainly consider it.
That could be difficult.
Maybe, I'll look into it.

The "yes" that is not agreement

When you hear "yes" from the other side, do not immediately believe that they agree with you. There are several different words for "yes" in Japanese, each with a different degree of strength.

Table 6.2 The different ways of saying "yes" and their rough equivalent meanings in English

hai	I hear you (encouraging you to continue talking).
So desu ne	I am still listening (encouraging you to continue talking).
Wakarimashita	Understood.
Tabun	Maybe.
Kekko desu	OK, agreed (this looks like you have an agreement, but it is wise to check because in certain contexts it can actually mean "No thanks!")
mondai nai	No problem; I agree in principle.

An interpreter is likely to translate any of these words or phrases as "yes", thereby losing all the subtly of the original meaning and this can easily mislead you. Note that the word *mondai* on its own means "a problem" but it is a weak word, which suggests that in this case a bit of care might be needed, rather than it being a full-blown problem in the Western sense. You should not necessarily worry if someone uses this word, but it is worth investigating just to see if they think it could be serious. If you can speak some Japanese you can listen for what word is being used to work out how much agreement is being expressed

You should never reject or refuse a proposal outright

If you do not like the idea, you can say you will consider it later, or perhaps say you will talk it over carefully with all of your colleagues. Any of the Japanese phrases to subtly say "no" can be used. Later of course you can refuse, but very politely, make an apology for it not being possible, and give your reasons. Be prepared to be tough – but with politeness and style. When the Japanese concede a point they do so as a magnanimous gesture – let them, and say you appreciate it. They will expect a concession back either then or later. You can usefully adopt the same tactics, which you can expect to work – you should not forget to push gently for a reciprocal concession for anything you have given up earlier.

It is dangerous to invent ball-park figures

You must be careful never to invent figures, engage in off-the-cuff statements or draw rough sketches, even as a simple example or to illustrate possibilities. You may well be used to winging it or flying by the seat of your pants during negotiations in the West. This is a very dangerous tactic to adopt in Japan and you should avoid the use of all ball-park figures. The team opposite will take careful note of the price, size or date etc., and what you intended as only a possibility for discussion may well be taken as a serious offer. Because there is a real danger that rough sketches may be taken as an accurate portrayal of your layout, product etc., not merely an idea, it is wise to prepare all drawings and overhead transparencies of your product, and anything that you think you could possible need before you leave home. If you must take unprepared action, you should keep stressing that it is an idea for discussion and not a proposal as such. They will still probably think it is a proposal that you are flying as a kite, and if later you suddenly say your idea is in fact a bad one, they are likely to wonder at your Machiavellian deviousness and might spend time trying to work out your hidden agenda!

Confusing the issue with logic

You should not rely too heavily on using Western logic when negotiating, and in fact it is far better not to use the word. The Japanese are not particularly impressed with the Western approach of a logical progression down a unilateral track. This seems simplistic and rather naive to them. Their concept of life is more complex: everyone exists within an all encompassing framework which includes both humans and the entire world of nature. Cause and effect are fully understood, but are seen as an overly simple and naive way of approaching the complex world in which we live.

Relationships go off in all directions, and things are bound together in a complex whole. As a result of this different way of seeing the world, any problem will usually be seen in the context of how it affects not only their department, other departments, and the whole institution, but also other companies, the industry as a whole, and the government. If you are discussing a specific problem and make what seems to you a sensible and logical suggestion to solve it, you should not be surprised if it is not immediately accepted. The Japanese will consider your proposed solution, but not in isolation, and will examine it looking for the impact on other departments, institutions, government policy etc., in a multi-stream framework. This will include not only the effects of what you suggest but they will also consider which individuals will have to be consulted or "squared" in the process. This different world-view often accounts for long silences from the Japanese after you make what seems to you to be a simple suggestion – there is a lot to consider as they see it.

You might find that they actually reject an advantageous suggestion, which they agree would be profitable, simply because winning over all these other people in their network would be too difficult or time-consuming to be worth the relatively small profit involved. They will rarely tell you why they turn the deal down; indeed they might find this hard to explain to a foreigner, who is unfamiliar with their thought processes and system. Many Westerners have puzzled over them turning down a good offer for no apparent reason.

Your slick presentation can mislead you

Do not feel that you are doing well or even winning easily, merely because you are presenting a well-argued case in logical fashion and it is not being refuted. The Japanese are singularly unimpressed by slick logical arguments. Many a Westerner has felt that he was leading the discussion and making a strong case that was being accepted by the opposite team which they could see was nodding regularly. Imagine the surprise later when nothing positive results. What has usually occurred is that the Japanese team was merely registering they were listening; it is normal for them *not* to argue or contest your points, but this does not mean that they accept them.

If you try really hard, establish a good logical case, and feel you are easily dominating and getting you way, be careful not to push hard for a decision. If you do, it is likely to strengthen their resolve not to give in and can easily lead to them offering fewer concessions rather than more. The principle of using your opponent's activity and strength to defeat him, while maintaining a watchful passivity is a central part of the sport of judo. It is an apt description of the negotiating style of some Japanese teams.

OK, who messed up?

It is important not place the blame on anyone else if things go wrong. This means that finding out who is to blame is not particularly helpful. The Japanese are likely to feel that it is not even worth trying to find out who was responsible for causing a particular problem, for in Japan this is really irrelevant. As team leader, or manager, your job is to put right what has gone wrong, restore the harmony and make people feel good again. It is not felt necessary to engage in detailed investigation and allocate blame. Note also that the person who caused the problem is not necessarily responsible for solving it, the person in charge is – in this case mostly probably you!

Don't send a boy to do a man's job

If a problem should arise, it is best not to send a subordinate to sort out the mess but do it yourself. Leaders are supposed to handle problems and not delegate.

If the problem is really major, it may be wise to try to locate a third party to advise you on the best strategy to adopt; or you might use this third party as a go-between to approach the other side on your behalf. Naturally such a person must be trustworthy and must not be a member of the unit with which you are dealing. If problems persist and you start to believe that relations are festering rather than improving, you should seriously consider using a local paid consultant and listen carefully to what they advise as the best course of action in your particular circumstances.

Problems are not examined in depth

If you have a problem, such as if you are forced to ask for a different delivery date, you need not explain why at great length. It is best simply to apologize, incline your head as you do so, and preferably accept personal responsibility for whatever has gone wrong. If, for example, the train was late so that you were not on time for a meeting, you can say it was late, but you should not blame the train or the railways but instead you can apologize for not having caught the earlier train. If shipping is delayed, you could say that unfortunately you chose the wrong seaport or shipping line, for instance. They will not believe this in any real sense, but such an approach is appreciated and shows sensitivity and you appear as a reliable and trustworthy person.

Best avoid the tempting gambit of blaming your Head Office

When the Japanese team indicates that they do not wish to accept a proposal of yours, it is definitely not a good idea to say something like "Head Office insists we do this". It is far better to discuss the matter and try to work it out. The Japanese will see your refusal to discuss the issue as demonstrating aggressive inflexibility and a lack of cooperation under what are clearly difficult circumstances.

In any case, blaming someone else is never polite in Japan. It is even worse to criticize your own company and the Head Office as this might be viewed as bordering on the traitorous, given the extreme loyalty given by the Japanese to their own company. If you really feel you have to do it, you might get away with blaming your HQ once during negotiations, but not more. Even then it would be better to suggest that it might be difficult for your HQ to accept, perhaps blaming yourself for not having the ability to persuade them, rather than say they insist on something.

Recourse to law is not the Japanese way

You should not threaten a Japanese firm with the law whatever the provocation. If you do, you could be forced out of the entire Japanese market, possibly for ever. The Japanese prefer to conciliate and strive for harmony, not litigate and end up in court. If you sue someone, even if you have an open and shut case in law and win easily, it is not only that particular firm which will never work with you again; your dreadful behavior in taking such action will rapidly become common knowledge. Networking in Japan is most efficient and the fact that you were right and proven so in court is irrelevant. You have committed a deadly sin, for which there is not now, or ever will be, forgiveness. North Americans, who take recourse to law more easily than some, should be particularly careful.

You must also avoid the extreme act of breaking off negotiations. If you were to do this, it would take a long time to build a fresh relationship with that particular company and it may in fact be impossible ever to gain their confidence after such a baleful act. In their eyes you have already demonstrated total untrustworthiness – would you trust your teenage daughter with a convicted rapist? Remember that in group-oriented Japan, if you break off with one company, the word is likely to spread quickly that you are not to be trusted and you might find your future approaches to other firms placed in jeopardy.

How to Behave When Presenting Your Case

A loud voice or behavior is a no-no
You should not raise your voice, lose your temper, shake a finger at anyone, or pound the table. In the West, such behavior is regarded with disfavor as too forceful and challenging but is far worse way in Japan, where it is simply unacceptable. In some Western countries, faking anger may sometimes be deliberately used as a weapon in negotiating but you should never adopt this tactic in Japan.

It is better not to look impatient or anxious
Emotions have to be kept private in Japan and children are taught to do this from an early age. Anyone showing anger, or even looking upset, is regarded as not merely unrefined but as demonstrating a weakness that is a sign of a hidden and serious character defect. It means that you are still so immature as to indulge in childish tantrums. Few Japanese would wish to be associated with such a person, whether in business or friendship, so that your effort to buy, sell, set up a joint venture, sign a trade contract, etc., would be put at risk.

Persistence and endurance are widely prized qualities; they are approved in Zen Buddhism, which allows for religious reward for physical feats of great fortitude. In Japan, you can watch rather bizarre game-show programmes on TV that involve a high degree of self-abasement, as well as extraordinary endurance to suffering discomfort and even extreme pain. The message of this for you is that you need to be steadfast if you are to achieve what you want, for they might try to wear you down.

Comparisons are odious

Remember that you should not openly compare your firm with others. Putting down a competitor of yours, or even mentioning one, is felt to be a crass and unacceptable way of self-promotion. It is particularly bad to use the name of a rival or competitor of *theirs* during negotiations as a lever to try to get what you want. This might sometimes be a useful threat in the West but would break a strong cultural taboo in Japan. It is often safer to pretend to yourself that the company with which you are negotiating is a single monopolist in the country and treat the negotiators accordingly. Generally, you should be aiming to persuade rather than manipulate, and cajole rather than threaten.

The way we are: descriptions of practices in your country do not always help you

It is tempting but generally unwise to explain how things are done at home and contrast these with Japanese ways. It will not seem relevant to Japanese negotiators and they dislike being lectured to, or hearing any suggestion that Japan is not the best. To their minds Japanese culture is clearly the finest, so not many have a serious interest in the peculiar ways of foreign countries. Naturally, if you come across someone who genuinely is interested and asks you about your country, then you should tell them. Even so, it is desirable to keep your answer short in the first instance and wait to be asked for more. If you do not get asked further questions, the questioner was probably trying to be polite, rather than sincerely wanting to know about how things are done where you live. If you do get in a conversation comparing behavior in your country and in Japan, always try to find something nice to say about Japan in the process.

Do not underestimate the opposition

Merely because they do not operate in the way that is customary in your society does not mean they are poor at their job. In particular, beware of deciding that someone is lightweight because they go slowly and do not appear to be dynamic or competent. The sort of person that the West sees as dynamic, talented, and possessing an immense capacity for work, often looks to a Japanese as a brash crude person with little authority now, and small chance of ever getting any. The cautious conservative person sitting opposite you plays to different set of social rules but he must be very competent to have got where he is and leading their team.

Humor is no laughing matter

You are strongly advised not to tell jokes or try to be amusing in any way. Humor rarely translates across cultures and what seems funny in one society is too often unfunny, and sometimes downright insulting, in another. It is particularly important to avoid making jokey remarks about the Japanese language and culture. The *Noh* theatre in particular lends itself to puns in English as does the name of the parliament (the *Diet*) – but forget it! Similarly avoid humorously using *Zen* for "then" in an English sentence. Do not make would-be funny comments about transvestites or AIDS when you encounter men playing women's parts in Kabuki theatre. Such things simply do not seem amusing and people are likely to feel personally insulted if they conclude you are being rude about their beloved country and culture.

When the team is on its own, or thinks it is, e.g., in a hotel lounge, you should try to avoid making jokes about Japan, or Japanese pronunciations, such as the common lack of distinction between "L" and "R", which can sometimes yield superficially amusing results along the lines of "erections", "flied lice" and so forth. If you are overheard doing this, it would alienate almost everyone; and in addition it might lead to your team inadvertently slipping into joke mode or suddenly smiling at a particular pronunciation of an interpreter in a subsequent meeting. This will be noted by the team opposite, who will resent your rudeness.

On a similar basis, when negotiating, it is important to avoid being facetious, sarcastic, or using irony. The interpreter will have trouble with all of these, and may not see there is a joke or get the point at all. The mangled translation that is likely to result might puzzle or unintentionally offend your audience. Once they feel that they have not understood something, it will be harder for them to follow the rest of what you have to say and they may be tempted to switch off completely. You might continue to talk on, thinking you are communicating, when no one present is actually following you at all.

Politely hesitant works well

In general, you should try to be politely diffident in manner at all times in meetings. This is true even if asking for what is clearly your right, or putting across an essential point for your side which you regard as nonnegotiable. A dignified reserve is prized and respected while plain speaking is regarded by Japanese as crass, unhelpful, and not designed to move the process of negotiations forward. It is also unwise to issue an ultimatum, as many Japanese would understand this as signifying the end of the discussions and that you are washing your hands of the whole thing. The only time to use this tactic is if you genuinely are about to pull out, cut your losses, and go home unless you get what you are asking for.

Body language – posture matters much in Japan

It is a good idea to keep an eye on your body language in any foreign country, as it can easily offend people from another culture. They will interpret your body language in their own terms and as a result they can totally misread your position. In many Western countries, standing or sitting formally has rather tended to die out and we are apt not to place much significance on posture. In Japan, such things matter a great deal. The Japanese are a formal people and can be surprised, confused, or feel insulted by a sloppy appearance.

You should always try to sit in a formal upright position and with your feet flat on the floor. It is better not to cross your legs if you can help it, as this is considered very rude in the presence of a superior and some Japanese will think it provocative and challenging. It can also expose the sole of the shoe, which is itself not desirable.

It is a good idea to study the way the Japanese are sitting or standing and follow their lead. You might be surprised how upright they sit, as if in trained in an army to sit always to attention.

Desperately seeking patience

While you are listening in a meeting, sit still. It is important not to pick fluff or lint off your clothing, or do anything like doodling, sketching, playing with your pen, fiddling with your jacket buttons, or searching your wallet or briefcase for things.

All such habits tend to be seen in Japan as demonstrating a lack of sincere interest, as well as being downright bad manners and immature. Try not to fidget, however bored! You are under constant scrutiny and even an action such as you repeatedly crossing and uncrossing your legs will be noticed. It is important to be seen as patient, for impatience is a weakness and they might try to exploit it.

Are you a standup guy?

When standing, a stiff upright posture, like a soldier on parade, is quite acceptable when first meeting - and even desirable. If however you persist with it as the relationship develops, then your stance might be considered impolite, arrogant, and perhaps almost threatening. A progressive relaxation can be adopted, but you should only go so far and try to remain respectful. If you can manage "stately" you will do well.

Not only should you avoid slouching, you should also not lean on walls or the furniture as this gives a very bad impression. If you stand talking to someone with your hands in your pockets you will be regarded as a rude and slovenly person. Some Westerners have developed this habit when they feel relaxed so keep an eye on your personal habits.

In the West, standing with your arms folded when talking to someone may indicate you feel defensive or maybe a bit cold. In Japan it is seen as being a very threatening attitude indeed, deliberately intended to rebuke the person you are addressing. This is definitely one to be avoided.

Looking at eye contact

When talking to anyone, you should avoid maintaining steady eye contact. In many Western societies, looking someone in the eye is taken as a sign of honesty, sincerity and integrity. In Japan it is considered belligerent and challenging. If you keep looking at your opposite number firmly in the eye, the person will first become uneasy and then might start to feel anger, although this will be hidden from you. It is particularly important that the members of your team do not stare fixedly at the other team's leader or try to hold his eye. Their status is lower than yours or his, and they should certainly not be challenging him. What you should do when talking or listening is to glance at the other person, then look down or look away. If you are doing the listening, then as you snatch a quick look at them, it would be beneficial if you nod, grunt, or say "yes", "surely" or "fine", which would encourage them to continue and make them feel comfortable with your behavior.

Some Japanese body language

Japanese body language is less obvious and harder to read than in most Western cultures. It is not only a matter of us being less familiar with their body language, which we are, but also a product of their training. In a typical Japanese family, the children are trained from their early years to conceal their emotions and maintain an impassive facial expression, as well as to maintain a formal body posture, or "stand properly". By the time they are grown up, most Japanese have been well trained to give nothing away. They have also had a lot of practice in minutely observing other people who are concealing their thoughts, and then deciphering what is going on behind the mask. This is one reason that they are often quick to detect a false note if you pretend to be interested in something which actually bores you, or say you support a view when you actually do not.

Body language is extremely culture-specific, and any books you have read or courses you have attended in the West will not apply to people from a different culture. It is worth understanding a little about Japanese body language because it will help you assess the negotiating situation better. You are advised not to adopt their gestures, in part because you might get it wrong, and in part because you are tipping off your hand that you understand what is going on.

If a Japanese negotiator sucks in breath through the teeth with the head slightly cocked to one side, it often means that something important is going on. He or she is thinking intently about something that they find intriguing. Perhaps what you ask is impossible for some reason they are aware of but you are not. Maybe what you have just said has caused them to feel that you have identified a weakness in their case, and they are trying to think of a way round it.

Should you encounter this behavior, think very carefully and try to work out what sort of important matter it could be. While not in itself negative, it might eventually lead to a concealed "no".

Another easy body language pointer is if the person you are addressing takes a sudden sharp intake of breath; this often indicates "no", without any words being spoken. A sudden tilt of the head when listening to what you are saying can also mean a hidden "no". General unease with what is being said may be signalled by a hand being placed on the back of the neck. Leaning well back in a chair can signify disapproval, whereas leaning forward suggests interest, just as in many Western nations.

An unusual but important point that you might come across is in the physical indication of oneself. In the West we tend to point to our chest, perhaps lightly tapping it for emphasis as we talk; this is in contrast with the Japanese, who point to their nose instead, which at first looks a bit odd to many foreigners. The main reason why you need to know this, is that pointing to the chest in Japan is a very aggressive gesture and is used to issue a challenge (not unlike Tarzan and his chest-beating in old movies) so you must try to avoid pointing at your body. If you see someone placing their palm flat across their chest, rather than pointing, it indicates a sign of confidence that they are able do something, perhaps in response to a suggestion by someone.

When someone in the West is perplexed or thinking about something deeply, they tend to scratch the back of the head and perhaps run their fingers through their hair. In Japan, it is the ear rather than the head that is scratched to show puzzlement and thought. When you encounter someone scratching their head in negotiations (and it is not just a sudden itch, which they would normally ignore) rather than simple contemplation, it may mean they are trying to conceal some clumsiness or weakness on their part, or else they are accepting that you have won the point.

Making a circle with the forefinger and thumb means something quite different in the West and Japan. It is best to avoid using it. In most Western nations it means something like "OK", "Thank you" or "I agree"; in Japan it simply indicates money.

If the person wants to say they have no money or the price is too high for them, they may wave their hand about, in a negative cancelling-out gesture.

Another piece of Western hand movement that means "OK" is the thumbs-up gesture; in Japan this has a totally different meaning and indicates a boyfriend. Now using this one could get you into real trouble! To indicate a girlfriend, the little finger is raised rather than the thumb.

Hand gestures are not really considered to be polite by well bred people and you should in general try to avoid them when negotiating. The differences in their meaning might however make a good topic of conversation when socializing, especially after everyone has had a few drinks and is relaxed.

If during negotiations you observe your opposite number tightening his eyes slightly then release them, it may indicate antagonism which he has immediately sought to conceal. Similarly, if you notice his top lip straighten momentarily when listening to a proposal of yours, it usually a negative sign.

Another possible indication of antagonism is if someone stands with the shoulders squared – but since a formal posture is required in Japan, it may be hard for you to spot the difference at first. Watch for a change in posture and the sudden movement that gives away concealed feelings, especially if the person looks even more formal afterwards.

Another common hand gesture, which signifies "no", is fanning the hand back and forth across the face or higher body. It rather looks as if the person is fanning away a bad smell assaulting their nose. It is a sign of rejection.

In the West, other than total body positioning, we tend to look at faces and eyes for telltale signs. This is often less useful in Japan because of the training since childhood to conceal their facial emotions and the preference for not staring. Perhaps the most expressive part of many Japanese is the hand; it is there that you should look for tension and inadvertent movements. You will probably encounter Japanese women raising their hand to their mouth to cover it when embarrassed, as if trying to stifle giggles.

When the Japanese present feel acutely embarrassed, they might retreat into uncertain laughter, so you should not assume they are amused but look to see if you have said or done something which could be offensive. However, laughter encountered when drinking and socializing is more likely to be genuine rather than not.

Persuasion beats pressure

Generally it is wise not to apply open pressure on the Japanese – you are likely to do far better if you try to win them over instead. Open bargaining and horse-trading, especially if conducted in a straightforward Western manner, often embarrasses the Japanese, making them feel insecure and uncomfortable. Calm explanations with an almost apologetic figure dropped in at the end are a far more acceptable way of making your pitch. Remember also that facts and data impress a lot more than your claims and opinions.

This Is What We Find

Confidences are not respected

There is no such thing as telling something in confidence in Japan so that you should never believe that anything you tell someone on a confidential basis will remain a secret for long. Any new proposal of yours will be spread throughout the work group as a matter of course. It would be unthinkable for a Japanese to deprive his colleagues of information merely because a foreigner told him it was confidential and swore him to secrecy. The loyalty to his primary group far exceeds any relationship that you might have developed with him on a personal basis. You may be able to use this cultural group trait to your advantage, for instance, if you wish to pass a message to a person on their team, but to do so in an indirect way, tell somebody else about your own level on their team and you can be sure that he will pass it on.

Reports are routinely made, circulated and discussed

You should assume that after any meeting, even a social one, there will be a written report about what was discussed which indicates stating your attitudes to the issues; this report will be circulated round the entire group. It will pay you to be wary at a social engagement if anyone on the opposing team casually mentions a subject that is currently being negotiated or will shortly come up; the person may well be trying to gauge your opinions and reaction. If they suggest that, in their opinion, someone on your team opposes or favors something, they may well be on a fishing expedition for information to be used in future meetings.

The Japanese are very good at intelligence gathering, and their obsession with facts and details means that they are adept at organizing reports from a variety of sources and then collating them at a central point for future use.

Keeping to the agenda may not be on the agenda

You should not be surprised to find that an agenda does not exist or, if you are given one, you should be aware that it might well be jettisoned early or be totally ignored from the start. Meetings are often not run on Western lines proceeding from item to item in logical fashion and indeed in Japan their purpose can be different. A meeting may simply be to strengthen a relationship; or announce what should happen; or rubber-stamp what has been argued out and agreed elsewhere between the interested parties. In a meeting, every Japanese professional knows that they are there to listen closely, perhaps but not necessarily discuss alternative solutions, and strive towards a consensus. Strong argument is sometimes allowed but only after this is signalled as acceptable. In many meetings hardly anyone speaks because the people present understand it is the appearance of democracy not the reality that counts. Negotiating should result in an agreement acceptable to all, and preferably look as if there are no obvious winners and losers, even if there really are. The Japanese will take as much time as is needed to achieve such a result.

They hated my presentation – didn't they?

A good presentation is often received in silence. You should not feel upset if this happens to you, for it is not a criticism. In the West you would expect to receive congratulatory smiles, or words expressing gratitude for such a lucid and logical presentation. The Japanese are more likely to sit quietly and mull over what you have said, considering the immediate implications, what might be involved further down the track, who outside the room should be informed, and what this would mean for favors they are owed upon which they can draw. In addition they will probably be considering how true a picture you have just painted, and how it fits in with the information that they already possess. They may also wish to discuss it among themselves and work out the team's position and devise a common front before responding. Few present would dare indicate their views until they know how the group as a whole feels.

Does price matter?

If you are trying to sell consumer products to the Japanese, you should be aware that until very recently, consumers have tended to choose the best quality, and whatever was currently fashionable, seemingly with little attention to price. The "best" item might in fact have been identified as the one which was the most expensive. Around the year 2003, some 40 per cent of sales of the world's luxury goods went to Japan alone. Until recently, "No name goods" or own-label brands were not generally accepted by Japanese shoppers who preferred top quality goods of beautiful design and with immaculate packaging. Imported consumer goods of luxury status or snob appeal are highly sought after and the main brands are known and clearly ranked in Japanese minds.

A change began in the early 1990s when Japanese shoppers began to behave more like the Western textbook "economic man", and become more price-sensitive. Discount stores have opened up and now offer a strong challenge to the legions of small "Mom and Pop" shops and to the existing high-quality-high-price department stores. Discount stores have introduced new methods, including buying abroad, bypassing the (very inefficient) traditional distribution systems and offering goods at low prices. This has been successful; consumer prices fell which helped to increase the standard of living despite the low rates of economic growth during the nineties.

Another recent change includes a growing preference for once-a-week supermarket shopping and greater use of refrigerators, rather than the traditional daily visits to the small family corner store and buying for immediate consumption.

Japanese cartels and monopoly arrangements

There are many monopoly arrangements and restrictive practices in Japan. Unlike those in the West, where they are generally a simple desire to maximize profits, Japanese restrictions are closely related to the culture. As you know, upsets to the general harmony are widely disliked. This means any new brand or company that is trying to break in will usually be criticized, and someone will allege "excessive competition", simply because it will force change upon existing structures and relationships. Cartels are often allowed to continue to exist because they maintain orderliness and prevent prices from altering. Even consumer groups have been known to support cartels and accept the need to pay higher prices in order to keep harmony and stability. Such cartels and monopoly agreements certainly create problems for foreign competitors, but that is not their sole reason for existing, despite international criticism that they keep foreigners out.

It is a good idea not to criticize the cartels, as it will do no good and tend to alienate those you are trying to get along with. In any case, the cartels are getting weaker as time goes by.

Once you have started negotiating, the top man in the Japanese company usually cannot help you

Once negotiations have commenced, it is rarely desirable to raise a suggestion with the top man in a Japanese company or ministry. You will probably embarrass him, because that is not the way things are done, and in any case there is little point, since he is no longer involved. His function is to set broad policy and then leave the nuts and bolts work to the people below, and they then have to consult widely to get things approved.

If you have an idea or proposal to present, and you are not yet deep in a series of meetings, you could explore the company from the bottom up. Remember that it is preferable to approach several layers of management, because of the *nemawashi* system. If meetings have already begun, then that is where you should raise your idea; or you might choose to float it outside the meeting on a drinking-social occasion and wait to see what happens.

The attitude towards contracts can be cavalier

It would be unwise to expect that contracts will be scrupulously honored. When times change, a Japanese company might easily ask for a contract it had signed earlier to be suspended, altered, or simply ignored. It seems ludicrous to a Japanese business person for anyone to insist that an old contract be followed under these new circumstances. At heart, the Western concept of the sanctity of the words of the contract is lacking. Rather the spirit, sentiment and meaning of the contract is regarded as important, not the legal formality. Between friendly companies, managers would regard it as wrong to insist on out-of-date and empty words if, for example, exchange rates or international prices were to alter substantially. They prefer to rely on the spirit that inspired the contract in the first place and quietly adjust things.

Consequently there is little point in waving a signed contract and expecting that simple act to settle the issue. If you are a partner in a joint venture and do not see eye to eye with your Japanese partner, an appeal to the words of the original contract is not likely to work. Further, they might think that you are obliquely suggesting the parties might end the agreement - which could throw a large spanner into the works. A refusal by you to help out in some way when requested and a rigid insistence on the actual terms of the original contract will always incense the Japanese. A little flexibility by you would be appreciated, and you could consider suggesting something you want in exchange for any concession you make.

Hey, I can ask for a contract change too!

Do not forget that you can ask for contract changes. There is nothing wrong in taking advantage of the culture which allows pleading for special treatment under changed circumstances. If for instance your costs have been forced sharply up since you signed a long-term supply contract, you could ask for a price increase. Under similar circumstances, the Japanese would probably ask for one. Put aside your ingrained attitude towards contracts and suggest some modification. If you do not act as they do, then it becomes a one-sided event whereby you are permanently disadvantaged. Few Westerners ever seem to take advantage of this golden opportunity, because we too are victims of our own culture with its idea of sacrosanct contracts and the rule of law.

If you are selling internationally traded primary produce to Japan, the prices tend to vary constantly and the Japanese are torn between liking stability and wishing to reduce costs. If they should ask for a price reduction (perhaps below the prices stipulated in the contract, because international prices have fallen), as a tactic you can use their argument and point out that you favour stability, harmony and long term relationships. It would be difficult for them to reject, because it is a central element in the culture. If on the other hand international prices should rise and you are supplying on an old contract, remember that you should forget your Western legal attitudes and consider asking for an upward price adjustment.

A few of the younger and more Westernized Japanese are starting to regard contracts more in the Western way, but they are still in a small minority and you would be well advised not to assume that you will be dealing with them. At present they are generally too junior to have gained sufficient responsibility to have more than a slight influence on outcomes.

Harmony: really only a means to an end

You should not be taken in by the idea that in Japan *all* is compromise and harmony.

Much has been said about the desire for compromise and harmony in Japan, both here and in other books, but you should not believe that this is any more than socially desirable. *It is really only the method of operating, and is not in the prime goal.* The goal is simple: it is to win. The Japanese love to win and despite going through consensus and compromises, in the end they wish to gain the main advantage, preferably while concealing the fact that they are trying to do so or have actually succeeded. They stay in there, slugging away but ever so politely, and so must you. Remind yourself that they rarely if ever will be merely enjoying your company – they are constantly working towards victory.

Selling primary produce is easier

If you are involved in straightforward negotiations to sell simple primary produce then your work might be a lot easier. Much of the advice above on negotiating tactics applies to complex and difficult deals that might take a long time to set up and bring to fruition. With a simple, standardized product, the price is often the only real consideration. Without a domestic supply of almost all the raw materials that they need, the Japanese have been buying them for a long time and there is virtually an established way of doing it by now.

Despite this, the attitude often persists that the buyer is king and sellers are a somewhat low form of life. It will pay you to exercise care and behave properly in Japanese fashion, as it can save you time and money by speeding up negotiations and shortening your stay. And the next time they want to buy, it might by your firm that they feel the most comfortable with and so approach you first. It would pay your company to ensure that your negotiating team is sophisticated and does not include highly knowledgeable but "rough diamond" types who may possess great work experience but lack the polish necessary to avoid upsetting the team opposite.

In standardized raw material negotiations, one danger that you might face is that the Japanese will combine representatives from various companies into a team and negotiate with you as a monopoly. They often try to do this, and then use their collective muscle to negotiate a lower price. They will then use their success with the first supplier to squeeze lower prices out of other foreigners, who are of course your competitors. Japan as a whole benefits from this process and the foreign supplying nations collectively lose.

After You Return Home

Reasonably soon after you have got back to your base, you should write a letter of thanks to every single person who extended hospitality to you or who did you some kindness, such as providing you with a useful introduction. It is customary in Japan to write letters simply to maintain a relationship, even if there is no real reason to contact the person at all. If you type your letter it has something of a remote business feel about it – but if you write it by hand it is more personal and hence preferable. This small act of sending a letter couched in simple friendly language can help you to succeed.

In addition to your "thank you" note, if you add all your contacts to your Christmas card list it would also assist your future business prospects. You should make sure to write a note in it yourself (i.e., not by your secretary!) in order to personalize it. Few Japanese are Christians (around two percent of the population) but they do like to celebrate the festive season.

It is customary in Japan to send cards for holidays other than Christmas, especially for the New Year. It will pay you to send them to lots of people. As for Christmas cards, you should personalize each card with a specific comment or two which indicates that you have a genuine concern – a signature alone is never enough.

Seven: Subsequent Negotiations–Their Methods

Attitudes towards Time

Slow down, details ahead

The other team are likely to take their time and move slowly during the negotiations. The Japanese tend to spend far longer discussing details before reaching agreement than most Western business people would consider normal or even useful. It often seems that little is being achieved and what seems to you to be a minor issue may take weeks to resolve. You must be patient when this occurs and keep fighting any feelings of frustration. However, one consequence of the Japanese approach is that once agreement is reached and the contract signed, they are often ready to move suddenly and at a rate that can surprise you. If you are not ready to start in a big way, virtually as soon as the agreement is signed, they will be disappointed and may even start to doubt your sincerity and wonder if maybe you are having second thoughts about the deal, or are inefficient and unfortunately incapable of reacting quickly when needed.

The whole approach is opposite that common in the West, where it is normal to begin by getting a quick broad agreement, commence the job, and then expect to deal with details and problems as they arise. This culturally different attitude towards a project is often a source of frustration for both sides. Remember that they are dealing with an alien culture too.

Their silence is often golden

Do not be surprised if the meeting sits in silence for considerable periods of time; if this happens try not to look at all impatient or annoyed. The Japanese are comfortable with silence to a degree that is rare in Western countries.

There can be several reasons for the silence. If you have just made a suggestion, the Japan side may sit quietly pondering over it and you should wait, not breaking the silence even if it goes on for several minutes. It is not a negative event and they are usually carefully considering what has just been said, including any ramifications for others not at the meeting who will have to be briefed and perhaps persuaded into line. The other side will respond when ready.

A second possible reason for the delay is that everyone is waiting for their leader to say something and in hierarchical Japan they feel constrained to keep quiet until he breaks the silence. The superior person present is the only one who can initiate a conversation and it would feel wrong for any other team member to start up.

Thirdly, silence may also be used by the Japanese as a weapon, while they sit and watch the impatient foreigner squirm, so that they obtain a psychological advantage. In Japan, silence is widely believed to give strength and power, and its use can be seen in the glowering and posturing that occurs between the two contestants in a sumo ring just before the wrestling actually begins.

Finally, in discussions there seems to be a need for empty space that serves some perhaps not very obvious purpose, just as it does in the arrangement of Japanese gardens or in calligraphy.

The demand for time out

It is common for the Japanese team to suddenly ask for time out to discuss among themselves. Such tactics often do not mean much and they should not be considered as ominous or threatening. This is especially so if you have made a suggestion that they had not anticipated. Recall that their agreed position has been cleared extensively with others and any novel suggestion from your side might need a careful review by this team to see if they have the power to deal with it there and then or if they need to clear it elsewhere, and if so with whom.

Their Behavior

Are they falling asleep?

Do not be surprised if some of the team with which you are negotiating close their eyes while you are speaking. Some Japanese business people prefer to close their eyes completely while others merely allow the lids to droop slowly, leaving the eyes half closed rather like a cat. Such behavior does not indicate sleepiness or boredom but is a common Japanese habit. Some Japanese claim they listen better that way. However, you might recall that Japanese do not believe in staring into someone's eyes, as this is considered challenging and rude, and closing their eyes solves the problem of where to look.

In the extreme case, you might find the senior person opposite actually does fall asleep! This can be a good sign as he clearly does not feel the need to monitor what is going on, because he feels things are going well and can be left to his juniors to handle. If you encounter this, it is usually best not to make an issue of it but simply pretend it has not happened.

Whether awake or not, their closed eyes meant that they are not seeing your body movement and gestures. If you are accustomed to use body language deliberately to influence people, it will not work when no one is watching! And as you will recall, such body language rarely transfers across cultures or even worse, it may carry an unintended totally different message.

Big Brother is alive and well: you are being watched

Remember that you are under observation at all times. In formal sessions and outside them the Japanese will observe you and your team carefully in order to assess how effective you are as a leader and how united is your team. They are constantly probing for any weaknesses in your armour that they can use to their advantage. It is important for your side to be seen as a unified team and not argue in public or reveal dissension in the ranks. Try to get your members not to interrupt each other or to criticize, even gently, what one of your team might have said. If possible, the individuals on your team should not even offer minor amendments or corrections.

Of crucial importance, no one on your team should ever interrupt the leader, either yours or theirs. This may be difficult to achieve with a group of Western individuals, but do your best. The Japanese will interpret any interruptions and corrections as indicating a loose team which is ill-prepared and of low ability. They will almost certainly try to use any information they gain about who favors which proposal, or sides with whom, as future levers to gain what they want.

If you feel a need to change goals or tactics or offer a new concession, it is better to ask for a short recess and discuss this within your team in private, before returning to present a united front. It is usually a good idea to ask for a break anytime anything comes up that you have not previously considered and discuss this with your team, so that internal debates are not observed by the other side.

Questions, questions

Do not be surprised when you are asked many specific detailed technical questions – remember to bring all the data that you think you might need with you. If you are unlucky enough to be caught out in something, you can immediately tell them that you will produce the information as soon as possible, then fax back to your HQ immediately after the meeting and mark the request top priority. A quick response impresses the team opposite that you are trying hard.

In the West you might table a technical document and let them read it carefully later on but in Japan you are more likely to be asked to read out technical specifications first, even for some considerable time, before tabling it. They enjoy listening to detailed facts and accumulating specific information, just as they tend to dislike hearing generalities and opinions, once the early formal general sessions are out of the way.

Leaders come and leaders go

You can expect that the leader with whom you are dealing may suddenly change. After an initial polite query reveals he is not unwell etc., it is best to accept the situation quietly, and not keep enquiring after the missing person's whereabouts. It is part of the opaqueness of the Japanese system and difficulty of identifying real authority either in companies or the country as a whole. It is extremely difficult, some would argue virtually always impossible, to find out who has the clout to change things or even make a decision. After one thinks one has identified a power center, the nebulous chains of influence often tend to shimmer and dance then dissolve away into nothing. You are not alone in finding this difficult – the Japanese themselves complain about it also!

You might find that their side will conduct the negotiations using a reasonably senior person as team leader, and then suddenly bring in a really important person to finish off and sign. If you are suddenly faced with the production of a really big gun in this way, it may well mark the commencement of the closing stages of negotiations. It may also cause you to be forced to concede more than you had expected, as it is time for the last "sweetener". Note that the team leader with whom you have been dealing all along may not be the person who will make the ultimate decision and he may not even finish off the series of meetings, but leave the task to someone else

The ultra-friendly contact may not be all he seems

You should be a bit wary if you are given a particularly friendly and extrovert Japanese contact. A Japanese company may well use such a Westernized, outgoing, and helpful person, usually fluent in English, to keep you occupied but without advancing your cause. Such a person normally has very little power within the Japanese firm. His job is to keep you happy but not to do business. If you find you keep meeting someone like this (especially if he is on his own) but nothing much seems to happen in the business negotiations, then you should suspect that you are being fobbed off and the company is not really interested in what you have to offer but is too polite to say so. The higher and more important men are usually reserved and quite self-effacing; they rarely appear as extroverts or are the kind of people that foreigners can easily relate to easily. They do not often speak really fluent English anyway.

Their Tactics

You go first

During the negotiation process, the Japanese team will usually let you speak first while they maintain a reserved position. They prefer to sound you out and learn as much as possible about you and your position, before they reveal their own hand. Because they have done their homework and investigated you and your company before you even met, then gathered as much information as they could both in and outside the official meetings, they are often in a stronger position than you when the negotiations of substance begin. They certainly try to be. The effort that they have put in probably makes them feel more comfortable about their negotiating position than you do and gives them additional strength.

They tend to be counter-punchers

You may notice a tendency for the approach of the Japanese team to be reactive or defensive rather than initiators. They will probably have carefully worked out several ways of defending their preferred position but they may not have clearly thought out ways of persuading you to their viewpoint. This is often a weakness of theirs. You can expect them to be well prepared, know what they want, and defend it obstinately. They are less likely to be creative and push into new areas.

Although they are often not that good at countering your ideas

Few Japanese negotiators have a tendency to think in terms of debating points one after the other in Western style. Despite being experts at defending their position, they are frequently not adept at working out the possible strategies that you might adopt and then deciding what to do about it. This means that they sometimes find it difficult to counter an offer or suggestion immediately. If you spring something on them, they might dig in their heels or ask for a recess.

They do not bend much - except when bowing of course

During the negotiating process it is common to find that your position is a lot more flexible than theirs. They usually have less power to make decisions and may sometimes need to stop a meeting and refer back. Alternatively, they may choose to drag out the meeting without reaching any conclusion, because they are really stalling until they can check later with another person or group. The lack of flexibility is because their team has already managed to achieve decisions with several other departments etc., and they know that any major concessions they are forced to make to you will subsequently involve them in a whole round of extra *nemawashi* negotiations. They wish to avoid this and it tends to breed stubbornness on their part. You can, however, assume that if their leader agrees with your request or position, he will try to push it, should they be forced to go back and reconsult.

Good guy, bad guy

You might encounter a "good guy-bad guy" approach, where one of their team ignores harmony and enters the argument forcefully, to be followed by a sympathetic person who attempts to restore harmony – and gently pressures you to make concessions in order to achieve this desirable goal. It is all done by prearrangement on their side of course. You might get somewhere by (nicely) suggesting a compromise from them, or you could try immediately switching to examining the history of the negotiations to this point and showing how well they are going, and restore harmony that way.

The "foreign goods are inferior" line

During negotiations, you might be told that foreign goods are inferior. You might even hear that for some reason (perhaps strange or even patently ridiculous) they do not suit the Japanese market. If you meet this, try not to get annoyed or express strong disbelief. If the claim is really outrageous, keep a straight face and do not smile derisively or laugh. In part this is nationalism speaking, but quite genuinely the Japanese consumer often prefers Japanese goods. Things like motor vehicles really are well made. However, as a protective device, officials will often invent excuses, such as the imported good is the wrong shape, or of lower quality, or is dangerous owing to different health regulation abroad, or it contains unacceptable amounts or types of insecticides etc. The government once banned the import of skis from France, with the excuse that Japanese snow was different from elsewhere!

Kevin Bucknall

The case of rice has often been sticky. It has long been heavily protected by the DLP in order to keep the farming vote. Myths about the product abound: for instance, a lot of Japanese do appear to believe that foreign rice does not suit their digestive system and will make them ill. Apart from that, many Japanese seem prepared to keep out foreign rice even if it means they must pay a higher price. This is partly because Japan is, or at least was, a rice culture; the green fields and seasonal changes reveal the relationship of man to nature and there is a strong emotional commitment to such things. Rice is a special commodity for one more reason – in historical times the samurai were partly paid in rice in lieu of salary in the Tokagawa Shogunate. Further, in modern times, the rice fields have acted a bulwark against urban sprawl and industrial pollution. Finally, the common feeling of isolationism and genuine fear of being cut off from foreign sources of supply lead to a widespread acceptance of the goal of self-sufficiency.

Goods such as beef, which is heavily protected, are felt to be much less important culturally so its continued protection does not have the same degree of general support. The Japanese are still not big meat eaters as traditionally they ate rice, vegetables and sea food and meat was actually tabooed for over a thousand years before 1868.

"You've simply got to help me!"
If you have done well in the negotiations and are clearly ahead of the game you might be subjected to a technique called *naniwabushi*. This is a strategy, traditional in Japanese culture, which involves metaphorically throwing oneself at the feet of the opponent and begging for mercy. The person pleads strongly, virtually grovels, and claims that he will be so badly affected that he will be destroyed. Should this happen, you will be seen as responsible for the downfall. In Japanese society this tactic is often effective and some concession is both expected and usually given.

This tactic may appear as you are getting towards the end of the bargaining process and you will need to make a small concession at this point. If you refuse a concession under these circumstances, it can push a Japanese negotiator's back against the wall. His response might be to feel that the situation is hopeless, and the whole negotiations might as well be abandoned.

In principle you could also use this general tactic of *naniwabushi*, but it is difficult for a foreigner to indulge in such self-abasement. If you are game to take it on as a tactic it, you should remember that it is something of a last-ditch event and must never be used early in the negotiating process.

It's easier once you are established

The Japanese might well make friendly concessions to you if you have an established pattern of doing business with them. They are often willing to look after old business colleagues and make a compromise that would probably have been refused earlier. In effect you have become a part of the "family" and this may merit you special treatment. The better treatment of those they are familiar with is another reason for persisting in looking for a long term relationship, rather than going for a quick "in and out" profitable deal. Although it can vary, it might take you around five years to achieve such a status with a Japanese company. You can use your status to suggest that your history of long cooperation between the two companies might be marked if they were to offer something you want, but it must be done obliquely and politely, not in blunt fashion.

All animals are equal

You need to establish a relationship of equality with the Japanese side. The Japanese see themselves as honorable and moral, with a strong feeling of conscience, *but this is only the case if they feel they are dealing with equals.* The honorable attitude, and the behavior that follows from it, tends to be far less powerful when they are dealing with an inferior. This is because in a hierarchical society the inferior is supposed to defer not to argue. This is one reason why it is so important to choose the strongest team and the correct local representative. It also means that once you have established a good relationship and are seen as an equal, you might find that you can appeal successfully to the conscience of the Japanese team leader should a problem arise for you. This is less likely to work if you are in a new relationship. An appeal to honor and doing the proper thing is always worth trying, but do not attempt this before you have been accepted as a friend and equal.

What if their tactics suddenly change?

It is usually significant if the Japanese team abruptly changes tactics. If negotiations have been proceeding for some time, then you observe that the Japanese team has unexpectedly changed their approach and begun to adopt Western negotiating tactics, i.e. they are suddenly remarkably direct and perhaps even aggressive, suspect that you may have a problem.

It could be that they think that the negotiations are getting nowhere, they are feeling desperate, and they are trying this last ditch approach. They would rarely make such a change for preference: the Western approach frequently goes against their basic cultural beliefs, and they are aware that they are not particularly good at Western-style negotiations. If you encounter this event, even if you believed everything was fine and you were doing well, it should be taken as a signal that something may be seriously going wrong. Stop and think carefully about where the problems may be and try to tackle them. Otherwise, rather than winning, there is a danger that the whole deal might suddenly collapse on you.

If you are ever subject to violent language

Should the Japanese team leader suddenly explode into violent language you have a serious problem. Everything said above about harmony and consensus becomes forgotten. He may have begun to feel the talks are fruitless, your behavior appears to be insulting, and, as he sees it, you know nothing about how to behave. He feels that the situation is intolerable, and you have gone so far away from civilized behavior that nothing further can be achieved. It is to be hoped that you never encounter this problem, but if you do he is probably trying to punish you for what the Japanese side as a whole regards as some heinous offence.

If you are unfortunate to ever encounter this, you should say as little as possible. Whatever happens, do not try to laugh it off or treat it as a joke. The best thing to do is ask for an immediate recess and at once seek the assistance of a professional consultant. If you cannot sort this one out, you face the danger of not only losing the contract or whatever but also ruin your longer term chances in Japan as a whole. Other firms and ministries will quickly hear about it, and they would hesitate to do any future business with you. You're in the last chance saloon and this fact is being clearly signalled to you.

Eight: Socializing and Proper Behavior

Hospitality is not the same as friendship

You should be careful not to confuse hospitality with friendship. Much entertaining is done and enjoyable times had in groups but this is part of normal business practice and does not signify you have suddenly made a lot of friends. The person hosting the evening and with whom you are drinking and getting along famously might not actually be a friend of yours and could even be actively opposing you behind the scenes. There is a clear distinction drawn between gregarious enjoyable behavior in groups and strong personal friendship. Do not let yourself be softened up by the extreme hospitality, for you are likely to be treated as royalty, and you should guard against making extra concessions out of a feeling of friendship. Remember also that being *treated well* is not the same as *doing well*; your competitors are probably receiving exactly the same treatment, yet only one foreign company might be in line for the contract.

Similarly, good manners and extreme politeness are a necessity of the cultural system and do not necessarily denote friendship or even a feeling of goodwill towards you. Politeness is demanded for its own sake but does not signify much.

Friendship can be sincere but it will be limited

If you try hard, are sympathetic to the culture and possess a degree of luck, you can become good friends with many Japanese to a degree which will make you happy. You can become close friends but you are unlikely to achieve the status that another Japanese could; the Japanese regard foreigners as fundamentally different and you might notice that they rarely marry non-Japanese. You may find that you are complimented upon your ability to speak Japanese and eventually feel that you "belong" – but from the Japanese viewpoint you will remain something of a talented outsider, however long you live in Japan, and no matter how well you speak the language.

You will meet some expatriates who have lived in Japan for years who will assure you that they themselves are now fully accepted and integrated. They manage to hold this view, despite probably being aware that those Koreans or Chinese who look exactly like the Japanese (some, but not all, look different) and whose families have lived in Japan for generations are still not fully integrated. They still

135

cannot achieve Japanese nationality, nor are they fully accepted socially. Before marriages are agreed, the other family is often investigated by private detectives, mainly to ensure that they are really Japanese by blood and not Koreans or some other nationality regarded as inferior. If people who were born and brought up there, look the same, speak the same language, eat the same food and so forth are still considered outsiders, what chance does an obvious Occidental have?

Gift Giving

The Japanese constantly give gifts to each other

Giving gifts occupies an important place in Japanese culture – both the giving and the receiving of gifts demonstrate that one is a member of a group and reinforces the group strength. Choosing gifts should be done with care. They must be of high quality and chosen with care for their suitability.

Note that all gifts *must* be wrapped, or they may not even be identified as being a present! Receiving a gift imposes an obligation to do something for the giver so that when you receive one it is wise to make a return gift as this offsets the obligation. If you do not keep giving presents in return, you will find that your obligations mount up and at some stage they will probably be called in. You might then be asked to do something that you might prefer to avoid.

What to do about that expensive gift

If you have received an expensive gift or are unsure what to buy in return, it is best to seek local help. You should make sure the value is approximately equal to the one received. Be careful to spend time choosing a suitable gift because what you give matters very much. Major international brand names are well known and their merits are carefully rated in Japan, so choose a well-respected one. The *relative* values of gifts you supply are crucial – you must give the most expensive one to the top person and reduce the cost as you go down the line, carefully grading the values. Be prepared to give a gift to the top four or five people with whom you are doing business.

Gifts and your first visit

On your first visit to Japan it is wise to have small gifts with you, especially if you are trying to sell rather than to buy. This shows sensitivity and good manners on your part and as we all know, selling is generally harder than buying!

A small gift that strongly suggests your company would be acceptable, and it might usefully carry your logo, to act as a tangible reminder of you and your firm. Scattering a lot of these around now may pay off later. The gifts might be typical of your country or state for instance too.

On subsequent visits you must bring gifts

You must bring a gift for virtually everyone you met last time, to demonstrate the relationship is good and going forward. If you receive a gift at any sort of gathering on this trip, you will be expected to reciprocate at the next meeting with a suitable present. You really need plenty of items with you, just in case.

Gifts made in a third country are not a good idea.

You should ensure that anything you give which represents your country is actually made there. In particular, it must not have been made somewhere else in Asia like Hong Kong or Taiwan. It should not be made in Japan either, as this would indicate you took little trouble or gave it no prior thought. This means buying plenty of gifts in your own country and carrying them with you.

Institutional gifts and personal gifts

In the institutional/business world, gifts are often expensive and impressive. Depending on the event, the institutional present might vary from an expensive work of art (if for instance opening a joint venture) down to more mundane items like pens, paperweights and T-shirts, preferably with your company's logo on. If you can get them made out of special local wood or other material that either your company or country is well-known for, so much the better. You need small gifts for those with whom you are negotiating and you can place them on the table by their chair. If it is one large and impressive gift to the company then you can hand it over, with suitable modesty about its lack of worth, when their key players are present. An alternative way with a clearly corporate single gift is to hand it to someone you know the first time you see them, making it clear that it is to the company, department, etc., and asking him to see that it is given. When you have a set of gifts, one for each person at the meetings, it is a good idea to hand them over in the first meeting.

With personal gifts, what is felt acceptable and desirable is subject to change, almost like fashions in clothing, and it is wise to check with locals what is regarded as suitable or is highly prized this year. A good well-known brand of whiskey, such as Chivas Regal or Johnnie Walker Black Label (not Red which is too mundane), is generally acceptable. By all means use your duty-free goods, but get them wrapped carefully before handing them over. "Coffee table" picture books depicting your part of the world are always pleasing. It is better to avoid things like perfume, aftershave or handbags, as they feel too personal for what is a rather ritualistic occasion.

Let's wrap it up!

There is a great symbolism attached both to gifts and to the paper in which they are wrapped – both should be appropriate. For the wrapping at least this usually means both expensive and tasteful; if you use a poor quality wrapping paper you will go down in their estimation. The packaging is best done professionally. If you wrap it yourself, do so very painstakingly and in an expensive way, using high quality impressive paper. Never use white or black paper to wrap a present in, as both can symbolize death, or red which is reserved for truly joyful celebrations. Green, grey, beige and blue are fine and in general darkish and formal colors are best. You should avoid all childish looking patterns and remember *not* to put a bow on the gifts you give, as this would look very strange to the Japanese.

Ceremony and deprecation

You should present your gifts ceremonially while at the same time apologizing for the insignificance of the gift. You can say something like "It is only a trifle", "It is really nothing at all", "I feel ashamed that is so little", or "Just a very small token of our esteem". Gift giving is fun and expected in Japan, but some foreigners find the self deprecation expected and the association of good manners with being humble a little difficult to adopt. If you feel a bit silly or insincere in your protestations just remind yourself that you really need to buy, sell, sign the agreement or whatever, and this is part of the price of doing so. After a while you will probably find that it does not seem out of the ordinary and you can manage it easily.

Open your gift back at the hotel

When you are given a gift in Japan, it is considered rude to open it in the presence of the giver. You should observe this rule, unless you are pressed to open it at once. Some Japanese realize that in the West we usually open them up and then make a thing about thanking the giver. They might adopt our custom when with you, although it seems strange to them. When you give a present to someone, you should not encourage them to open the package, which would appear crass. They will thank you at a subsequent meeting for any gift and if you received one you must not forget to thank them effusively later. Almost all Japanese bow as they say "Thank you" and it would seem to them most unnatural not to do so; if you incline your head as you express your thanks, it would please them.

Four and nine are nasty numbers

For superstitious reasons, the Japanese do not like receiving gifts in units of four or nine. Four has connotations of death, because of the sound in Japanese and nine denotes suffering. Be careful not to give boxed soap, for example, if packed four to a box, as can occur in the West. Five is a much more acceptable number and considered to be a set. Generally speaking all odd numbers (except nine) are generally better than even ones. Seven is a good number and has connotations of Buddhism, and forty-nine (seven squared) is also good. Thirty-three also has a good feeling, because Buddha can transfer into thirty-three bodies. Ten, despite being an even number, is also good, and symbolizes perfection or completeness, rather as it did in the American movie of the same name.

Certain items are a no-no as gifts

A knife should also be avoided as a gift, as it symbolizes the cutting apart of the relationship, as can anything particularly sharp such as scissors or even a paper knife. Chrysanthemum flowers should also be avoided as they are associated with funerals, and older people in particular might be reminded of approaching death. Flowers are probably best avoided as a gift anyway, as they are seen as either too personal and rather romantic or else connected with illness and death. Many bunches of flowers are designed purely for funeral use, and *should* you choose to give flowers, you should be careful not to buy funeral ones accidentally. It would not be well received, especially if the person you give them to is no longer young! If you feel that you really wish to give flowers, you could ask in your hotel for someone to write down that you want the flowers for a gift and not for a funeral then show it in the shop to be on the safe side.

You must never refuse a gift

This would be a dreadful insult to a Japanese and quite unforgivable. When receiving a gift, a small show of being undeserving and pretending to be reluctant is considered polite before you gracefully accept it. You should never refuse any invitation either, even if you have to rearrange your schedule or departure date to fit in. The rewards of accepting the invitation can be great, but the loss caused by a (seen as offensive) refusal can be even greater.

The even-handed approach

You should use both hands to give or take a present, not just extend one arm. Half a bow, little more than a slight inclination of the body as you extend your arms, would make the gesture complete. It is always polite to use both hands when receiving or passing anything to anyone and you should make a practice of it. People may not particularly notice when you do, but they will always notice when you don't.

Giving by rank

In Japan, a status-conscious society, people tailor their gift by the rank of the person receiving it. It would be wrong to give the same present to people of different rank: remember, the higher the rank, the better the gift should be.

Not again!

It is important not to give a person the same item twice. To do so would indicate a lack of interest or respect for the other person and a rather cavalier attitude towards both the person and the company he works for. It is a good idea to keep a list of what gift you gave to whom and when, so that the next time you visit Japan, you can look up what you gave last time and choose something different. Do not forget to update the list each time you go back. The exception to the rule is for high quality spirits such as whiskey and brandy, particularly if they have indicated that they like a particular brand. Repeating that gift then shows care and forethought.

If you go to a weddings or birth celebration

It is unlikely that you will be invited to a Japanese wedding or birth celebration, as foreigners would be felt out of place, but if you do, remember you must take a gift of money. The amount tends to depend on who you are, who they are, and what your relationship with them is. It would be best to make quiet enquiries among Japanese colleagues or friends about what would be a suitable amount. Your interpreter might be helpful here. It is essential to make sure that the notes are perfectly clean and uncreased – brand new notes are best. If you are stuck, some banks have a machine that cleans and presses banknotes to make them more acceptable to customers. Money as a gift must always be given in the proper envelopes that you can buy from stationary stores. To ensure you get the right kind of envelope you can explain in your hotel why you want it and they will write the proper characters for you to show in the shop.

Living in Japan, means gifts galore

If you are working in Japan, you should be prepared to exchange presents on a regular basis. You must reciprocate whenever anyone gives you a present, e.g. a friend or your next door neighbor. Note that it is normal to take a gift when visiting people in their homes, and if you do not do this it will always be critically noted. If you were Japanese, the lack of a present would probably be considered a deliberate insult; as you are a foreigner it will be put down to foolish ignorance.

Such gifts are expected to cost much less than institutional presents or those for your important business associates. You will of course be buying the gift item locally, but it still should be from a well-known and expensive store and be wrapped in their own instantly identifiable gift paper.

There is a seasonal rhythm to the giving of gifts, with a midsummer period (*Ochugen*) and a year-end one (*Oseibo*), both of which neatly coincide with the receipt of bonuses at work. The year end is the main gift-giving period, starting around December 10. There is also a bit of a seasonal bias in the type of item given: in summer, a suitable gift might be kelp, whiskey, dried mushrooms or fish; vegetable oil; or perhaps condiments. Prawns and bream are also traditional gifts. Speciality imported foods usually make desirable gifts. A good soap is a popular gift, but many families have become overstocked so that it is less valued than in the past. The situation changes of course and enquiring locally what people are giving this year is a good idea. Many gifts get recycled, so if you give chocolates to people who happen to be allergic it does not matter as they will simply pass them on to someone else.

Drinks after work and sporting invitations: it's party time!

When invited, go go go!

You must accept all invitations to socialize. Socializing is an intrinsic part of doing business and refusing an invitation would be a major insult as well as leaving the Japanese side not knowing how to proceed and probably slowing down your negotiations, resulting in a longer stay for you.

Where will you go?

You are likely to be invited to dinner, go for a drink in bars, or asked to visit a cabaret and you might find you are invited out several times during your stay. It is normal to go out straight from a meeting to socialize, often with little warning. Drinks and dinner are probably the most common invitation. When you get there, it would be courteous to allow your host to select your meal for you. Business should not be discussed while eating, but you might find your host raising an issue afterwards. This is often used as an informal way for Japanese to sound out business partners, without commitment on either side. After dinner, it is customary to go on to another venue, and *really* start drinking and enjoying oneself. Weekday evenings are often reserved for business entertaining and are not generally regarded by managers as private time.

Oh, I'm not sure ...well, alright then

It is really polite to make one refusal before you accept *but* do avoid the word "no". When receiving an invitation it is considered polite to say "It would be too much trouble for you" before you gracefully accept. Do this, rather than immediately saying "Thank you very much, I'd love to", as you might in the West. If you issue an invitation and receive the rather odd sounding response of "Never mind" in reply, this is a way of saying "no" (which is not really meant and the person really means "yes"), so that you should persist with your invitation. As you are aware, hidden meanings and polite phrases abound in Japan. After a while you will probably start looking for hidden meanings too, and ultra-politeness may start to take hold of you also. If you have lived in Japan for some years, you might find that when you return to your own country, that people look a little askance at your acquired excessive politeness.

Socialize for success

The successful conclusion of your business may hinge upon your socializing properly. Although discussion of business will rarely be directly undertaken while socializing, it is an integral part of doing business. Your willingness to participate and be friendly will be carefully noted. You are expected to enjoy yourself, relax, and get drunk, and you will be watched to see if you *really* like Japan and the people you are mixing with or whether you were merely pretending earlier when you were sober. Socializing together is complex mixture of bonding and friendship along with business, as they learn what sort of person you are.

You might be surprised at just how much people drink. They may also behave in ways that seem a bit childish to you, rather like young college students determined to have fun. Unless you are an experienced drinker who can cope with large amounts of alcohol, you might consider pretending to be a bit more drunk than you really are and go with the flow. Those who remain sober at drinking sessions are considered to be party poopers and are not admired.

The drinking ritual

While people's glasses are being filled, it is most important that you do not start to drink but wait until everyone has received their drink. If you start in earlier, it is seen as insulting or disparaging to the others and this could easily delay the group bonding process.

One of the oddities is that *you must never fill your own glass* when drinking, but wait for someone to do it for you. When this occurs, you should at once take a sip appreciatively and perhaps give them a little nod, as this is a way of thanking them for the courtesy. Not to take sip at once but to wait until you actually wished to drink would be seen as insulting and indicate that you care little for the person who served you. Whenever you are served in this way by a colleague, you must offer to fill their glass in return – remember to do this, as again a failure to do so is very rude. Note that if drinking alcohol, it is polite to touch or hold your glass whenever someone gives you a refill, not leave it on the table.

It is a good idea to keep your eye on the glasses around you – remember that they too are not allowed to fill their own glass. As they finish their glass, you can seize the bottle and pour for them; otherwise they will mostly opt to sit there thirsty rather than help themselves and appear gauche.

If you happen to be eating when someone serves you something, it is customary to stop eating until they have finished, as this shows them respect.

Sake, a rice-based alcoholic drink, is served warm. While the taste seems innocuous to many Westerners, reminding some of them of warm sweet lemonade, it is surprisingly potent, at around 16 percent. Many normal grape wines are around 11-13 per cent, so it is stronger than some might think, despite the pleasantly mild flavor. For most Westerners it is usually the quantity which is drunk rather than the intrinsic strength that can cause problems.

Singing for your supper – and other business

You should be prepared to sing one or more solo songs during the evening. After dinner, it is a common practice to go on to a karaoke bar, where people from the group will get up and sing something to pre-recorded music. It .is no accident that the karaoke system was invented in Japan; it is a natural outcome of the way of doing business with its socializing after work. The standard of singing achieved is often surprisingly high, which is the result of many hours of practice in private. You must participate and sing a few songs when asked to do so. A refusal would break the harmony and group spirit and could actually cost you the contract or trade agreement etc. that you seek. It is a good idea to carefully rehearse a few numbers before you leave for Japan, perhaps relearning something you knew in your teenage years, so that you know the words and music. If it is an old standard pop tune, or currently popular, the words might well be on the karaoke machine. You should know that there is great interest in rock and roll, blues, and jazz in Japan, particularly among the young. Japan has produced some fine musicians and in the pop music area it is common to come across a sort of fusion of Western and Japanese music.

The particular songs you choose might open up a conversation and help to bond your group with theirs. It pays to think carefully about the generality of the song as well as the words; something specifically associated with the Second World War for instance would not be a good choice nor would anything about militarism or denigrating Japan. If their group leader or company president has a particular interest in, say, a particular charity, then something from "Sweet Charity" might give you the chance to point this out; if he is interested in paintings or Van Gogh, then "Vincent" by Don McLean might work for you. You have to do careful homework to discover this kind of thing, but it surely improves your business prospects.

Other venues to go to after dinner in order to socialize and drink a lot include hostess clubs or night clubs – often terribly expensive.

The "Banzai" ending

At the end of the evening you might be surprised when everyone suddenly joins in a shout of "Banzai!!" three times. It is just a desirable way to end the evening, and amounts to "Three cheers for this great occasion".

Where are the wives?

You should never expect a man's wife to be present on social occasions, even if you specifically invite her. In Japan, women are not expected to play any part in business affairs, even at what might be thought of as essentially social dinners. At these, the group is often engaged in a friendly masculine bonding process. The woman traditionally stays home and raises the children while the husband goes out and earns the money to make this possible and to bring status to the family. Many men are "out with the boys" most evenings and rarely think of asking their wife – indeed the group would regard it as most peculiar if a member even suggested bringing wives along.

Should I take my wife?

For this reason, it is better not to take your own wife to a business-social gathering, if she was not specifically invited. You should take your wife to the restaurant only if the host is taking his, otherwise your wife might well find she is the only woman present, which would be disconcerting for her and she would feel out of place. Even if she is invited to someone's home for dinner, it is still wise to check before the event to enquire if she is *really* expected. The chances are your host was merely being polite and does not really want her to show up. Whether the invitation is serious or not often seems to depend on the degree of Westernization of the host. If you indicate that she sometimes has a tendency to headaches, for example, you might find an immediate suggestion from the host that she should stay in the hotel and rest as it provides the perfect way out.

The dinner to which you are invited may be intended to discuss business matters at some stage. Business is rarely if ever discussed in front of women, so that if you take your wife the Japanese will hesitate to raise a business issue, so that you may inadvertently negate the whole point of the invitation and slow down the negotiations.

If women do attend a party, you will notice that the women tend to gather together in their own group, the men in another. This is also common in Australia but less so in North America or England. Do not make an effort to mingle and join the wrong gender group thinking this will help break things up. It will merely embarrass everyone present.

Problems for a female leader

If you are a woman representative, you may find problems trying to entertain the Japanese. Outside Tokyo, many of them will not know how to treat you, as the situation may be outside their experience and they usually have little or no skill in dealing with high-powered female executives. It can be even worse if you bring a male partner along as a companion. The Japanese would automatically address him as the natural leader, but in this case he is not the boss. It is all most disconcerting for them (and see Chapter 11).

Personal questions

On social occasions, and sometimes elsewhere, you might be asked some questions that seem to you very personal indeed. For example you may asked your age, marital status, why you have no children yet, why you are so thin, or details about your career path. Requesting such information might seem strange in many Western countries but in Japan asking personal questions indicates a genuine interest in someone, and is intended to develop a friendly relationship. If you do not wish to reveal personal details, such as why you are not married yet, a vague and imprecise answer will do – "As soon as the right person comes along I will!" is perfectly acceptable. If asked "How much do you earn?", do not say something like "Not as much as I am worth!" as this would sound arrogant – stick to ambiguous answers like "Not a lot really", "A reasonable amount" or "Enough to get by" and you can immediately add "How about you?", which in turn develops the relationship (and see Table 11.1, pp.200-01).

You might find that the Japanese seem a bit less impertinent in their questions than in some other Asian countries, such as Hong Kong or Malaysia, where asking about your salary level or how much you paid for something you are wearing is common. Again, in these countries it denotes a friendly interest in your welfare. The degree of intimate detail asked in questions by some other Asians also tends to embarrass the Japanese. Cultures just vary on this one.

The great game of golf

If visiting Japan on business, you should be prepared to play golf and perhaps tennis. This naturally affects your choice of whom to send, especially since older people generally carry much more status but are often (although not always!) past their prime in the sporting arena. A fit middle-aged man would generally be a better choice for your team than a young athlete. Age has its compensations in Japan! Golf has become something of a ritual in Japan and you are being honored if invited to play. Golf courses are scarce and playing is incredibly expensive. Many golfers only ever manage to play on a driving range rather than on proper golf courses. To obtain a slot on of these, it must sometimes be booked weeks in advance.

Normally the host will greet you at the front entrance of the golf club, so it is important to be on time but best not to get there too early. If you happen to get there well in advance, I suggest that you hide around the corner. If you turn up twenty minutes early, the pressure on the golf course is such it is likely that a party of four in front of you will be waiting, the group in front of them will be just teeing off, and your host will not know what to do with you.

When you meet your host, he will show you to the locker room and usually give you a small gift – it is, as you see, a gift-giving society. If this is a box of golf balls, probably with his company's logo on, you must use these there and then, and not your own. Your host will probably encourage you to unwrap them for immediate use which is one of the rare instances of opening a present in front of the giver. Remember that you must never discuss business on the golf course unless the host starts to do so (unlikely). Expect to play the first nine holes, then take a long break for lunch; it is better not to query or comment on this habit but just accept it as the way things are done.

Table Manners and Dining Etiquette

As in many countries, there is quite a rigid etiquette about food and dining.

If it's on the plate it can be eaten

Normally everything served on the plate can be eaten, including any flowers or leaves - anything that you see. You should try a mouthful of everything offered, for politeness' sake, but you need not finish things you do not like. As long as you have tried a food item, it will not cause offence to leave it. If you know that you really cannot eat something, such as octopus, you can quietly indicate this well in advance of the meal, and the host will make sure you are not served it. You really should try to widen your palate if you can however. You should not criticize a food item you cannot eat, of course, but you can apologize lightly by saying something along the lines of your Western palate is unaccustomed to such delicacies or wonderful offerings. It is better not to use a phrase like "strange food"! Claiming an allergy is also acceptable but remember it may limit your food choice on all subsequent occasions.

When invited to dinner in a restaurant, the "best" seat is felt to be facing the entrance door and opposite your host; you might be seated there, but it rather depends on the relative status of those present. The chair at the end nearest the door is not regarded as a suitable seat for the powerful.

Seniority sits first

The most senior person present is normally the first to sit down so you should wait until invited to sit, so that you do not inadvertently offend the most powerful person at the table. If they insist that you sit first, they are honoring you.

Take care when asked what you would like to order

In Japan, it is polite to follow the lead of the most important person present and eat what they eat. As an honored guest, this again might be you and your decision can then rebound on a lot of other people. If you do not know much about Japanese food, you might order something inappropriate and face everyone with a dilemma. They are unlikely to tell you about your *faux pas*, but they themselves do not want to have to eat the Japanese equivalent of a Western bacon-and-egg breakfast in the evening in a smart restaurant. If you are a newcomer to the Japanese eating scene, it is best to solicit advice on what they suggest and ask them if the restaurant has any speciality that they recommend you should try. In this way, they assist you in choosing sensible dishes and you are also engaged in the bonding process.

How to hold the cups and bowls

There is a special way of holding the cups and bowls that are used at table. If soup is served in a small bowl but without a spoon, you pick up the bowl gracefully in both hands and sip at it. As with drinking tea, (which comes in cups without handles), you place the right hand around the cup or bowl and support it from underneath with the left hand. Picking up the soup bowl in one hand to drink is regarded as rather gross, especially for a woman, and should be avoided. You might see some males not using both hands, perhaps feeling it more macho, but you should use both. Where one hand is used, it is normally the left one. If in any doubt about the way of holding a bowl, it is best to watch to see how someone else picks up a bowl and copy them.

When eating from a bowl using chopsticks, you hold the bowl in your left hand in order to free the right hand for the chopsticks. It is polite to have four fingers under the bowl and the thumb resting lightly on the top. It is considered bad form to hold a bowl underneath with both hands and with the fingers pointing forward, because it looks as if you are begging which has a nasty feel about it. Remember that you should not make a joke about what you might see as the peculiar way of having to hold things or the different foreign eating habits you observe, as it definitely offends people even if they smile at you.

Help, there's no napkin!

In some Japanese restaurant you might find that no table napkin is supplied and you are expected to bring your own. It is a good idea to carry several large "man-size" paper tissues to use instead. If you forget, then you can spread your handkerchief on your lap when seated. This is often the main use for a handkerchief in Japan, apart from discreetly mopping the forehead on hot steamy summer days. You might find it useful to carry a second handkerchief in reserve for this purpose but you should note that many Japanese regard handkerchiefs as somewhat unsanitary. You will probably be given a hot towel both before and after the meal, in order to wipe your hands; some men also use it to wipe their face, but this is not considered ultra-polite. You are expected to fold it carefully after use; this is part of the general passion for neatness and rules governing the way you are supposed to do many rather mundane tasks. Place the used hot towel on the tray or by the side of your plate if there is no tray.

There are few communal dishes to worry about

Unlike the Chinese who virtually always serve food in a communal bowl to be shared by all, the Japanese traditionally serve an individual meal, often on a tray. On this, you will find the rice bowl, with lid, standing on the left, and soup bowl, with lid, on the right. You start by picking up the paper-wrapped chopsticks and pulling them out. Do not crumple the paper, but instead tie a knot in it, and then place it on the right. If you are given disposable wooden chopsticks, you have to separate them where they are joined at the end; you do this by pointing them upwards and pulling gentle apart. You should then place them on the chopstick rest if there is one, and if not put them on the paper you knotted earlier. They should be parallel with the table edge i.e. across your place setting.

The process of eating

It is good manners to start with the rice; lift the lid with the left hand and put the lid down on the left of the rice bowl and facing to the right. You do the same with the soup bowl, but use the right hand and place the lid on the right of the bowl facing in. The two lids should then make a symmetrical pattern with their respective bowls. It is considered rude to eat anything from either bowl without picking the bowl up in the left hand. Eating begins in a strict order – first you take a mouthful of rice and swallow, then next a mouthful of soup, and finally back to the rice for a mouthful. After that you can eat in any order you chose but a mouthful of rice is often used as a palate-cleanser between other morsels of food. Note that it would be considered definitely eccentric to finish everything in one bowl before moving to another. These rules may seem strange to foreigners, but that's the way things are.

As indicated, the Japanese pick up the rice bowl in their hand and do not leave the dish from which they are eating on the table as we do in the West. There is a tendency to hold the bowl lower than the Chinese, who will often raise the bowl to the lips and scoop rice in. A really polite Japanese will often try to keep the bowl at around low chest level and then lift the rice on the chopsticks. Another major difference from China is that the Japanese try to keep the rice looking nice and clean, so they do not put pieces of food on the top of it which would discolour and sully the pristine whiteness. Similarly, it is not acceptable to pour soy sauce over your rice.

You might face a silent meal

Recall that eating is taken seriously so do not be surprised if there is little conversation at the table once the meal begins. It is best not to speak until spoken to, in case you disturb the reverie which would both disturb the group and annoy the host.

Hot ain't hot

It is a common Japanese practice to serve cooked food that is cool or even almost cold. This does not improve the flavor, but few seem to mind; perhaps the appearance of the food matters more than the actual taste. Expect to encounter this at some stage, and do not comment. Food is served when it is ready, so that not everyone's meal will arrive at the same time unless all are eating the same dish. The members of a group will often order the same dish however, which prevents any implied criticism of anyone else's choice and keeps underlings from ordering something regarded as better than the meal ordered by the boss. If your meal arrives first, it is polite to wait until urged to eat – then after demurring, gracefully give in and do so. With the different orders straggling to the table and much food starting off cool anyway, everybody's food would be stone-cold if they all had to wait for the final dish to arrive.

Careful with those chopsticks!

You will not be expected to be wonderfully dexterous with your chopsticks. What matters is the etiquette, rather than the skill. Breaking some of the social rules of chopstick use in Japan is perhaps the rough equivalent of sitting in a Western restaurant and trying to balance the fork on your nose. It looks bizarre and would certainly make people wonder about you! The basic rule to remember is to keep the chopsticks low and avoid gesturing with them. It is important not to wave chopsticks about when at the table, and many foreigners forget this, especially after a glass or two of *sake*. Remember also not to move a dish or other item on the table using your chopsticks. It is also poor form to hold chopsticks grasped in the palm of one hand (easy enough to do if you are trying to free up your chopstick hand to use for another purpose) as this is the way that samurai swords were held when fighting - it just looks bad.

Chopsticks and the common food bowl

Although most Japanese food is served in individual portions, on occasion, some communal dishes may be served. In a family, chopsticks can be put in the communal bowl but this is not done in public or with nonfamily members. You should first look for and use the serving chopsticks which should be present. If none are provided, then you must reverse your own chopsticks and use the blunt end to take the food. Take care if you have to do it, as this is often difficult for foreigners to manage and the food can be slippery.

In Japan, you select and take your own food

You should not take a piece of food in your chopsticks and offer it to someone else. Traditional superstition has it that it is the bones of your ancestors that are being passed along. This is in sharp contrast to Chinese habit, where it considered polite to select a particular tasty-looking item and serve it to someone else.

The left-handed chopstick eater

If you are left-handed, take special care when eating. The Japanese will not allow their children to eat left-handed for two reasons. It is thought of as individual and eccentric, and this of course is regarded as thoroughly undesirable; and it also has the practical difficulty that left-handers keep bumping their left-side neighbor's elbow as both raise food to their mouths. What normally happens then is the food flies out of both pairs of chopsticks! Do make every effort not to let this occur. If you are unlucky here, apologize at once for your clumsiness and do not try to turn it into a joke, unless the people present do so.

A place for everything and everything in its place

It is considered bad form to place your chopsticks across the small bowl from which you have been eating. While you are unlikely to do so, it is absolutely crucial that you never stick chopsticks point downward in rice and leave them there – this symbolizes death in Buddhist ceremonies and would almost certainly bring a shocked silence. I have actually seen this happen and it provoked general alarm around the table.

Those picnic chopsticks

Should you be invited to a picnic where thin, disposable wooden chopsticks are provided, you will normally have to snap them after you have finished eating. You should wait for a lead from the Japanese here – imagine if the chopsticks were *not* intended to be disposable! If you throw disposable chopsticks away unbroken after using them, the traditional superstition was that devils may gather them up and use them for various nefarious purposes. Rather like the Western superstition that one should not walk under ladders because it is felt to bring bad luck, most people in Japan do not believe the devil story - but they avoid throwing away unbroken chopsticks anyway.

Slurping noodles

When eating noodles it is not considered impolite to slurp. However, these days some sophisticated Japanese try to eat quietly, in the way of many foreign societies. Despite this, you will find lots of people still suck their noodles into their mouth with a loud and clear sound. This is regarded as normal, particularly so if you are a man, and there is a vaguely machismo and hence desirable feel about this way of eating noodles. Women are not expected to slurp noodles as it is not considered a feminine act. If you are male, you might try to make these slurpy noises at least once, particularly if someone else has already done so at your table just to keep your end up. Some Japanese actually express surprise that foreigners are able to eat noodles so quietly!

The host toasts first

If there is toasting around the table, the host will always begin it. Everyone stands up for a toast to make an event of it, as part of the familiar bonding process. You should be careful to ensure that you do not knock over bowls or a tray, for example, as you rise, especially if a sudden toast takes you by surprise and everyone is on their feet before you. It is surprisingly easy to have a minor accident, especially as the evening wears on and the tide of alcohol is flowing!

Praise the food, it's part of your ammunition

Note that the preparation, presentation and serving of food play an important part in the culture, and to praise the food, for its appearance as well as the flavor, is to praise an important part of the Japanese way of life. Homemade soup is regarded as a particularly good thing to comment upon favorably.

Many Westerners reach the conclusion that Chinese food is generally superior to Japanese, but is rarely as well presented or pretty-looking – but *do not say this*! Note that in Japan the occasion of eating is often more important than the food itself, and eating together is a part of developing the relationship further.

Eat slowly!

It is regarded as most impolite for a Japanese to indicate that he or she is hungry. If you eat quickly it looks terribly rude to the Japanese eye, rather like a hungry dog descending on a plate of meat and wolfing it down.

Finger food

Different Western countries have their own social rules about when it is permissible to pick up certain foods in the fingers and eat them, e.g., chicken legs. Many Japanese feel it is disgusting to eat anything at all in the fingers and will go to great lengths to avoid it. If you forget and pick something up from your plate to eat, expect to face a sudden hush – and whatever you do, don't compound the error by licking your fingers afterwards. This is regarded as *totally* disgusting. Use your napkin instead. Remember not to crumple it up afterwards, but fold it neatly.

People try to finish eating at the same time

When at table, watch the others and try to time it so that you finish eating at the same time as they do. It is expected that all will finish simultaneously, a small act but which yet again works to bond the group. If you are not good with chopsticks and are going slowly, be prepared to stop eating, even if you have not had enough. It would be awful if they all sat looking at you, suddenly revealed in your loneliness as a long-distance diner!

At the end of the meal you are expected to tidy up your place, and even this is not done haphazardly but in a socially designated manner. First you place your chopsticks neatly in the chopstick rest if there is one, or on the knotted paper in its absence, and put them horizontally, pointing to the left. Then replace the lids on your personal rice and soup bowls, (if they came with lids, which is usual but not inevitable), and then move the bowls back to where you found them. You should remember to thank the host for a good meal when it is over.

You are likely to encounter sushi, with its raw fish

Sushi is now popular in many Western cities and you may have already become used to it. If not, it is a slice of pressed cold rice with a sliver of raw fish on, and possibly some vegetable; the whole thing may be wrapped in seaweed. It tastes a lot better than you might think. It is eaten with chopsticks, first dipping it in soy sauce. If small enough, the whole thing is placed in the mouth at one go, otherwise you cut can it in half, using your chopsticks. Some Westerners have trouble trying to cut it without destroying it. *Sushi* bars abound, and you might get taken to one for a snack or as a special treat to show you an important part of the eating culture. As it is a particularly Japanese dish, you can easily win friends by eating and then praising the *sushi*.

The chocolate pudding that never was

Some desserts that follow the meal closely resemble chocolate in appearance – but sample them with care. They often contain red bean paste that tastes *really* different!

Hospitality must be repaid

After you have been taken for a big dinner or evening out, you should offer reciprocal hospitality. Many Japanese would like to eat in a really nice (i.e. expensive) French restaurant; your hotel may have one. Failing that, they would appreciate being taken to a good one elsewhere. You must ignore the high size of the bill you will undoubtedly receive and accept this as a part of doing business in Japan. If for some reason you are unable to repay the hospitality immediately, it is acceptable to offer to return the hospitality when they visit your country as long as there is a reasonable expectation that they will do this.

Remember not to blow your nose while at the table

This is considered to be even more disgusting than just blowing it in public. It is surprisingly easy to forget this, especially after few drinks, but if you blow your nose at the table, all the Japanese present will feel revolted even if they do not show it. If you really have to do it, first politely excuse yourself from the table, then go to the rest room and blow your nose in private. Most Japanese would prefer to sniff for hours rather than blow their nose before other people.

Talking with your mouth full

Surprisingly to many, in Japan it is not considered gross to talk with your mouth full and expose the half-eaten food to your companions. The first time it happens to you, try not to look disgusted and turn away. We are conditioned by our parents and society to think it horrid, but not all cultures find it so.

Do not ask for a doggy bag

Even if there is a lot of food left over, asking for a doggy bag or attempting to explain in words that you wish to remove the leftover food from the restaurant, is likely to cause some consternation. It is not customary in Japan to do this and you would be regarded as extremely eccentric for wishing to take the food home.

Waiter!, waiter!

To attract the attention of a waiter, you cannot merely raise your finger unless you happen to be in a large Westernized hotel, with staff well-versed in the curious ways of foreigners. It simply is not a way of attracting notice. Instead, you should raise your hand and flutter the fingers in the air. It is the motion that attracts the eye.

The traditional Japanese restaurant

If invited to a traditional restaurant you will observe some striking differences. For a start, there are no chairs, which you will probably find uncomfortable, unless there is a well under the table in which to place your feet. You will be in a private room and served by young women who will giggle and talk, as well as look after you. You are unlikely to be asked what you would like to eat and the food will just arrive at the table. *Sake* will be served and there is a complex etiquette involved which borders upon the ritual. When someone fills your small cup, you should pick it up for them to pour into. Hold it still! Given the relative sizes of the tiny cup and the large mouthed bottle, it is not easy to pour accurately. Spilling *sake* is regarded as very bad mannered, probably connected with its early religious origins. Lower status pours for higher status, so that you are being honored when your cup is filled.

Help! Someone just gave me his empty cup...Now what?

Do not be surprised if a person finishes his drink then offers the empty cup to you. If this happens to you, take the cup and hold it carefully while the original user fills it. Then you drink from it. This is a mark of respect to someone senior and is felt to be very flattering. There may be a container of water in which to rinse out the cup between users but don't bank on it. Individual cups can travel about the table in this way. Because some people, normally the most important, will accumulate cups it means that others eventually have none; when anyone runs out, they take a cup from the pile in the middle of the table. It is all very Japanese and once more there is a strong group bonding element involved. If you are lucky enough to be invited to such a drinking session, you must go and you must drink *sake*. You cannot refuse a drink, so expect that you will definitely get drunk, unless you have the constitution of an ox.

The constant heavy drinking when socializing on business and the system that forces the more senior ones to drink the most may explain the tolerance and wry amusement with which drunks are often regarded. In Japan, the drunks you encounter are more likely to be important people or perhaps even role models in society rather than Skid Row residents.

When Visiting a Japanese Home

It is uncommon to be invited to visit a Japanese home

There are three reasons why you may never get an invitation to a home. Firstly, Japanese housing conditions are poor, particularly relative to the affluence in consumer goods; many Japanese are aware of this and feel slightly ashamed that Japan cannot do better. Secondly, they often feel uncertain about how to entertain foreigners properly and they may feel worried that they might get it wrong – and this would be terribly shaming. Finally, in urban Japan, the home is really off limits to visitors and it is felt to be very much a private family thing. Even friendly neighbors in a block of flats are rarely invited inside, and people may stand at the doorway talking for extended periods without anyone feeling uncomfortable about the situation.

For such reasons, most entertaining is done in restaurants, bars, and nightclubs rather than private homes. Perhaps if you get to know someone really well over a long period of time, you will receive a home invitation, but you should not expect it or feel in any way slighted if an invitation is not forthcoming. If you are lucky enough invited, you should appreciate the honor that is being done to you.

Be on time!

When invited to a private home, it is important to arrive on time. Strict punctuality is still expected of guests by more traditional hosts, although a few Westernized Japanese are prepared to accept, say, up to ten minutes late. Get there exactly on time – it is not worth your while risking needlessly giving offence. Some societies have developed peculiar social habits about times of invitation and arrival, such as deliberately arriving fifteen minutes after the appointed time as this is regarded as polite. England is just such a case; if you arrive dead on the appointed time for dinner in a private home you just might find your host still in the bath! Thailand too freely exhibits "It is alright to be late" behavior and in Bangkok people might arrive up to forty-five minutes late, but the traffic really is bad there. If you are used to obeying similar "arrive-late" rules in your society, while in Japan remember to change your style and be punctual.

Off with your shoes and overcoat

A clear distinction is drawn between inside and outside, and different rules govern behavior in each. Overcoats should be removed *before* entering an office, as well as anyone's home. It is a good idea to do this before knocking or ringing the bell, to avoid being caught struggling out of the garment, which would leave your host waiting and rather embarrassed. You might choose to wear shoes without laces when visiting, as it simplifies removal, but if your host is a really high official or business person, and is also very conservative, laced shoes might be desirable as they are more traditional.

Shoes indoors are taken seriously: it is rumored that even burglars have been known to remove their shoes before proceeding about their nefarious business! If you are renting an apartment you should take off your shoes at the door and put on slippers. If you wear shoes at home and the landlord hears about it, perhaps from a neighbor, you can expect the owner to be very upset and he or she may well refuse to let the apartment to foreigners again. Another place you will encounter the shoe-for-slipper exchange is a traditional Japanese hotel, where it is normally done in the entrance hall. Incidentally, if you have very large feet you will find that the supplied slippers are way too small – you might consider bringing some with you.

Slippers and socks and shoes

Your host may offer you slippers to wear – if not you stay in your socks. Before leaving your hotel to visit, you should always make sure there are no holes in your socks and they are as fresh as possible.

Leave your shoes neatly by the door, with their toes pointing to the door, and put on the slippers if offered. While doing all this, remember not to turn your back on the host, as this is considered rude. If you are a man, you will probably find that the hostess rearranges your shoes even more neatly than you managed, and you should not show surprise at this. If you are a woman, you should try to be particularly neat when placing your shoes; as a female, extra tidiness is expected of you! Whatever your sex, you must avoid nudging your shoes into position with your feet (which again is rude), and must stoop down to arrange them properly, using your hand.

Slippers and mats, the twain shall never meet

Do not step on the Japanese mats in slippers. If the house has Japanese mats (*tatami*) on the floor, you must take off your slippers at the edge of the mat before stepping onto it, even if you have only just put them on. Shoes never get near the *tatami* of course.

There are special slippers for the bathroom area

If you go to the bathroom in the house, expect to take off your normal indoor slippers and put on a special pair that you will find by the bathroom door. When leaving the bathroom, you must remove them; they are strictly for use in the bathroom area only. You should place put them back the way you found them, so that they are conveniently placed for the next person to use. It is useful to carry a spare handkerchief or two on which to dry your hands, in case there happens to be no towel in the bathroom, but put it away properly before opening the door to leave.

Greetings are a main room thing

After you arrive you will be shown to the main room. You might get a brief welcome at the door but the real introductory session takes place in the lounge room where people are gathered. At this point it would be a good idea for you to refer favorably to some previous meeting with the host and thank him if he did any favors for you, however slight. This gets things off to a good start. The weather might come next as an introductory topic. Before you are invited to sit down you should also pass over the gift you brought (two hands!) with a suitable denigratory phrase along the lines of "just a small trifle".

When being introduced, you will start with the oldest person present, as this reflects their honored status. After that you can expect to be introduced down the line, by age, finishing with whoever is seen as the least important.

The kimono

You might find that your hostess is wearing the traditional *kimono*, as might the male host. If this is the case, do not register surprise; it is reasonably common to find the old ways of dressing surviving in the home. It pleases many Japanese to maintain the traditional customs and they often find it particularly soothing to the soul in the modern frenetic world in which we live. It will give you a topic of conversation later, and you could admire the way the room complements the clothing, and ask about the maintenance of traditional culture and its value today. A polite query about the local neighborhood and traditional values would do no harm. In the past there was a strong sense of local community, but in the more rapidly developed housing areas it can be weak and this is often regretted by the people living there. This is a popular subject for discussion.

The Japanese home

Traditionally, Japanese homes were rather stark and severe; an elegant simplicity was sought and achieved. The interior walls were often sliding partitions and these could be made of paper on a lattice framework, rather than more solid walling materials. Modern dwellings are often different, and look more like Western houses or apartments. Inside they are likely to be cluttered up with furniture and possessions: the effort to achieve a Japanese elegant simple purity often seems to have been abandoned in face of the glut of consumer goods that people possess and the small dwelling places in which to keep them all.

You should wait to be invited to sit down by your host

You should not just drop into a chair, even if you know the person very well and feel that you are close friends. This would infringe a major canon of polite behavior.

Where will I sit?

You might find that your seat will be in front of a flower arrangement, or some work of art. This it is considered to make a splendid background for the distinguished guest. You could glance at it appreciatively and nod and smile for a few seconds before sitting but it is best not to effusively praise the work of art (see below "Try not to admire a particular item", p.161).

You will perhaps be given the seat of honor, which as usual is the one furthest from and facing the door.

What if there are no chairs?

In a Japanese house you cannot automatically assume that there will be chairs to sit on. If you are lucky, the house will have them, but if the family is traditional, you might find that you are offered a cushion on the floor. As you are unlikely to be able to kneel comfortably for hours as most Japanese can, you may ask permission to sit cross legged in Western school-child style. Women are not allowed to sit cross legged so, if you are a woman, ask permission to sit comfortably and when this is granted you may swing your legs sideways alongside your body.

Please eat some more!

If invited for a meal, the family will probably keep pressing more food upon you as you eat. Even if you are hungry and would really like a little more, you should first decline gracefully. The family will then insist, after which you can accept. It is important to refuse the first time for if you immediately say yes please, it sounds greedy and unrefined.

When you actually have had enough, you will probably find it difficult to stop eating, as the family will keep insisting politely that you take more. You can equally politely keep refusing. Eventually they will believe you and stop. To indicate that you actually have had enough and are not simply being polite, leave a little food on your plate. If you keep emptying your plate or bowl, you are tacitly asking for more and they of course will carry on pressing you to eat!

"Please" and an inviting arm gesture is often used as an invitation

When a person suggests that you have tea, or something to eat, they often politely bend the body and stretch out the right hand and say "Please have some". A simple "Please" and an arm gesture are commonly used, for example when letting someone enter a room or lift ahead of you, or asking them to sit down. You can usefully do this yourself in meetings, in your hotel room, or in restaurants.

Whenever you offer something to someone you should always hold it in both hands – this looks very polite; offering or passing something one-handed looks casual to the point of rudeness. You should never of course pull out cigarettes or start to smoke in someone else's house or office without first asking permission.

Try not to admire a particular item

Once seated, you should admire the home, and the decorations and so on, but keep this at the general level. It is wrong to praise any particular item, such as a work of art, feeling you are complimenting the family. With all the indirect messages being passed in Japan, the owner may interpret your admiration as a hidden request for the thing and then feel obliged to make you a present of it. Once they offer it to you, it is too late to say no, as all initial refusals are taken as merely a polite phrase and not meant to be taken seriously. He is working within a system of a clear distinction between "appearance" and "reality" but you are not. He will then repeat the offer more insistently. Both you and the giver would be embarrassed by a sequence of insistent offers and refusals; you might end up having to take away some prized possession of theirs, and maybe even breaking up part of their collection. Persisting in your refusal would be extremely offensive, as it would be seen as you rejecting a gift, and even worse, one that you asked for in the first place!

"What lovely children"

If they have children, you can and should congratulate the parents and say how clever and charming the children are. Unlike in many countries in Southeast Asia, it is permissible to pat children on the head, although this might be best reserved until you know the child well. If there are any flower arrangements you should make a point of praising the beauty of the flowers and delicacy with which they have been arranged as this quickly sets a good mood and furthers the relationship. It is improbable that they would feel you were asking for a bunch of flowers!

Dinner guests do not usually talk to their neighbor

The dinner conversation will probably be general and you should not start a side-conversation with your neighbor. This normal procedure in the West would be regarded as unsettling in Japan and an action that prevents the group from bonding and feeling united in their enjoyment of the occasion. The senior people present tend to initiate the topics of conversation, while the most junior will probably only listen all evening. Starting up a private conversation would also be seen as insulting to the seniors who began the current discussion. Remember you should not interrupt anyone, but let them finish.

Asking "What do you think?" could cause some confusion

It would be a bad idea to turn to someone and ask what they think about the issue that is being discussed. This would upset their sense of ranking. They would probably feel that they are an inappropriate person to ask and your request could severely embarrass them. They are in a cleft stick: to speak up would be inappropriate and rude because they are not the proper person to comment, but on the other hand, not to answer you would also be extremely rude as you are an honored guest. In desperation, they might look down and giggle, unsure of what is the correct thing to do. This is a common reaction to a socially intolerable situation.

You won't get to see the place

Usually you will be shown into one room and not taken around and shown the whole house, as might be done in some countries in the West on this your first visit. You probably will not even get to see the kitchen, let alone the other rooms. Guests are welcome in the main living area, but the rest of the place is felt to be a matter strictly for the family. Do not offer to help clear the table or wash up which would embarrass the wife, whose job this all is.

Often at the end of the evening everyone leaves together

The group concept is strongly ingrained and normally people leave en masse, often surprisingly suddenly to a Western guest. Expect this to happen and join in the mass farewells. I remember being most surprised the first time it happened to me and I found myself in a long line of people waiting to leave, then thanking the host and his wife when I finally reached the front, rather like a reception at a Western wedding.

The "please stay" pleas

When you are ready to leave, the host will probably plead with you to stay longer. This is merely a polite phrase and is not really meant. You should ignore his pleading and politely say that you have to go. When leaving a dinner party, a Japanese will probably apologize for taking up so much of the host's time, rather than to express thanks for a lovely evening, as would be done in the West. You may choose to do the same. If you are the only visitor and not part of a long line of leavers, you should make a personal farewell to every person present and not just to the host and hostess. It is expected that as you leave you will remove the slippers and put them down neatly together by the doorway, facing into the room you just left.

Are they making sure I leave?

Expect that the family will accompany you well outside the door and wait for you to depart before going in again. They will probably wave good-bye and they might even bow their farewells to you. In Japan, it is considered very rude to make your farewells inside the door and then let the guest depart, in the common Western way. Such an abrupt dismissal would suggest that the host did not like the guest, the evening was a disaster, or the guest seriously overstayed his or her welcome and a rebuke is being indirectly administered. The constant passing of indirect messages which necessitates the clear distinction between appearance and reality can make Japan a tricky place in which to understand what is really going on!

Waving is done differently in Japan

The Japanese wave good-bye with a sideways motion of the hand, not forwards and backwards as in some Western countries. If you wave good-bye to someone who is leaving and use your normal hand gesture, this often looks to a Japanese like a clumsy signal for them to return because they usually beckon someone by waving their fingers with the palm of their hand facing downwards rather than upwards. Waving good-bye in your normal fashion might result in them coming back looking curiously at you and wondering what on earth you want; in turn, you will probably be puzzled as to why they are returning!

Thanking your host later

You must telephone and thank the host for the party or dinner. You should preferably do this the day after the event and say what a lovely time you had.

Expressing thanks is an important part of the social custom, and not to do so is considered rude, and might even be taken as a tacit message that you hated it and are registering a criticism for some insult or other that you received. Neither of these outcomes would assist you in your business dealings. You should also remember to refer to the event at your next meeting with the person and be glowing about how enjoyable the whole thing was.

The Japanese Tea Ceremony

If you are invited to a tea ceremony, you must go

The famous tea ceremony involves far more than drinking tea in a ritual way. It is felt to be a central part of Japanese culture, embodying simplicity, elegance, purity, understatement, and a minimalist formality. Going to one is not unlike attending a particularly impressive church ceremony in a religion that you know nothing about. As a spectacle it is interesting but some foreigners find it a little boring or perhaps even rather pointless. If you should feel this way, it is crucial to conceal the fact and praise the event afterward. You might find that the more you know about it, the better it seems. It will certainly be a fruitful topic of conversation in the more leisurely moments of your business negotiations.

You will be expected to make a donation to the host, but the money must be placed in the proper kind of envelope first – your hotel might have some, or if not stationery stores sell them. Check with your interpreter ahead of time as to how much would be appropriate and *do* make sure the notes are brand new and perfectly clean without blemish.

What will happen and what can you say?

The ceremony is held in a formal manner in a simple room, in a rural environment, with starkly elegant surroundings. The utensils are equally simple and severe. In the recognized beauty of the tea ceremony, the ambience counts for much, as do textures, light and shade, elegance of line and the balance among objects and the spaces left between. See if you can gain a feeling of a sombre, wistful, slightly sad but elegant beauty. When asked about how you enjoyed the tea ceremony, a few comments along those lines would be very well received.

Examining one's feelings about nature, or about some natural object that has been altered and improved, is a very Japanese thing.

Nine: Working in Japan

General Business Matters

Our man in Japan

If your company is of reasonable size, you should strive to keep a permanent representative in Japan. It might be tempting to feel that once the negotiations are concluded you can simply go home. This course of action could be dangerous, as the relationship between your firm and Japanese ones requires nurturing by personal contact and physical presence. Frequent trips to Japan are not a perfect substitute for this, although they are much better than nothing. An on-the-spot presence can also lead you to understand their position and foresee their likely negotiating tactics better, and may allow you to find any weakness or lack of unity in their team. This is particularly so if you are negotiating with a team that represents several different firms from the one industry. The Japanese often try to put up such a team, as it gives them strength and allows them to pick off a lone and desperate foreign company and get a good price or excellent terms. They can then use the results to bargain with other foreign firms. A local representative will improve your business prospects.

The compartments of life

The Japanese often view people and things differently, as if they are placed in separate pigeonholes. For example all foreigners are viewed as separate from (and inferior to) the Japanese. Children's games are often rigorously segregated by sex or age, and there is a clear and well-understood difference in status or grade between different companies, universities, schools, and even kindergartens. This strict compartmentalization goes hand-in-hand with the approach of the world being an interrelated unified whole, so life becomes rather like being part of a giant honey comb in a colossal beehive.

Your problems are my problems

If you have a company in Japan, you must take a strong interest in the problems of your customers. You will be expected to go and ask the companies with which you deal what, if anything, about your product inconveniences them. When you do this, you should ask for suggestions about how you could do better with the good or service,

165

the delivery, or packaging etc. In this way you develop a long term relationship with them, you can improve your product and marketing, and can often prevent issues from arising in the future.

Even if you do not open a company in Japan, your customer's problems should be of concern to you. You might consider approaching them, in person rather than by letter, and asking what could be improved. This act can easily give you the edge over your competition. Note also that the Japanese expect a high standard of after-sales service and are often prepared to pay higher prices to get it.

Declining manufacturing opportunities

Japan is no longer a good place to establish a manufacturing concern. The high level of wages and usually high value of the *yen* mean that it is hard to get your production costs down. The gradual opening of the economy to imports is also reducing quite a lot of retail prices and this makes it harder for manufacturers. For such reasons, since about the mid 1980s, the Japanese have increasingly moved their manufacturing sector abroad, mostly to Southeast Asia and China. The process is often referred to as a worrying "hollowing out" of the Japanese economy. As the *yen* fluctuates, a few firms have moved some productive capacity back to Japan during weaker periods, but over time the trend has been one way. The country is however a good place for service industries, which are expanding rapidly, particularly in the financial area. Until recently access to these by foreigners has been heavily restricted, but relaxation has begun. It is still not easy to get in, but the rewards can be great if you manage to do so.

Memos are not memorable

Do not be surprised at the low quality of many of the memos that float about Japanese companies. You are probably used to tight memos which are logically structured. For example, one might introduce a problem, give reasons for its existence, analyze alternative approaches to its possible solution, and present a recommended course of action justified by logical argument. Japanese memos are usually not at all like this. To Western eyes, the memos frequently look sloppy, ill-organized and not properly thought through. People seem to just put down the information in the order it occurs to them, rather than making any effort to organize it. The information will probably all be there, but you will have to do your own work sorting it out.

What looks to Western eyes as sloppy memos is a reflection of the culture, in which Western logic is little valued and plays small part. People are supposed to accept information and process it within the group or by themselves, not have a predetermined opinion put on it (and of course a higher leader might later indicate the preferred line of thought – meanwhile options are kept open). It would be a waste of your time trying to improve the quality of interoffice memoranda, as what you want (the Western approach) would not fit in with the organization, attitudes, or behavior pattern of the Japanese managers or staff.

Letters are filed with the envelopes they came in

There is a good reason for doing this. In Japan, the name and address of the sender are written on the envelope as a matter of course. But strangely, to Western eyes, the exact name and address of the sender may not go in the letter itself; a few months down the track it might be hard to work out what a letter on file signed by a Mr. Sato could refer to or perhaps even who he is or where he works.

Hey! Look at me, I'm busy!

In Japanese society people feel they have to seem to be busy and dash about looking important. Loyalty to the company and visibly demonstrating commitment to it demands such behavior. There is no tolerance of the laid back individual sprawling at a desk looking cool. You will be surrounded by bustle but you will find that not all of it is meaningful work.

Closing down is hard to do

It is difficult to close down a loss-making joint venture in Japan. To do so would involve firing people which is still difficult for a Japanese to accept, despite recent changes in this area. In a joint venture, your partner would be horrified at a suggestion that you might consider closure and, after the initial shock wears off, is likely try to try to find alternatives. He will still doubt your integrity as a business person however. If you are even considering suggesting a closure, you should not mention this to anyone in the company. You must accept the fact that you need local advice and seek help from a good resident consultant, who may be able to suggest ways of proceeding that are more acceptable. It might, for example, be possible to get the Japanese partner to prop up the joint venture for some time, perhaps by buying materials from one of its other companies at below market prices or selling to a subsidiary at a higher price than you are currently getting. Financial assistance from a bank connected with your partner might also be a possibility.

Distribution and Marketing

Distribution systems in Japan are generally poor

They can be small, fragmented, old-fashioned, inefficient, and costly. The entire network is not really capable of servicing an advanced economy and is in desperate need of a radical overhaul. The retail trade is dominated by masses of small shops which until recently had the power to prevent large stores opening and thus depriving them of livelihood. The situation is changing but there is still much to be improved. The poor distribution naturally increases the final price of goods and also tends to keep foreigners out, as the many small but complex systems mean that foreign business people cannot easily find a single institution or person to approach.

Can I distribute for myself?

If you are a manufacturer, you should not automatically expect that you will be allowed to handle your own distribution. The existing system will do all it can to thwart you, and unless you are a major international company, it will often be successful in this. The relationship between retailer and wholesaler, and between wholesalers, takes years to establish; in some cases they have dealt with each other for several generations. Your chances of breaking in are a bit remote. Note that once you settle on a distributor you are expected to stay with that one permanently and it may be difficult or impossible to make any change. There is little or no flexibility in the network. This means that you should take great care in selecting the group with which you will deal.

Distribution is getting easier

The distribution system began to open up during the 1990s. Some foreign companies have recently managed to bypass the creaking system and been allowed to import directly. This process is expected to continue. Major changes in retailing are underway, and these are especially noticeable in beer and alcohol sales which are increasingly being done via supermarkets and discount stores. The process should make it easier for all newcomers as well as the bulk retailers.

Vending machines are everywhere and work well

It is possible to buy a large range of goods from vending machines which are easily visible at night, for they are brightly lit. To list just some items, you can find green tea, beer, whiskey, *sake*, coffee, dried squid, hair tonic, socks, boxer shorts, rice, soap, and pornographic magazines. This is an area of distribution in which Japan really does excel, although some complain about the excessive use of energy of the machines. Oh! And if the machine suddenly addresses you, do not be shocked. It might be programmed to say "Thank you", for example – but in Japanese of course.

Japanese packaging costs more

Unless you are involved in really cheap and cheerful products, your packaging should be of high quality and look impressive. Your customers demand high quality and will often refuse to buy if the appearance is cheaper and unimpressive looking. Further, there is often a long distribution chain for retail items, which can easily mean damage to the packaging. Few stores will accept goods for sale unless the package is perfect because they know their customers will not buy them unless it is. Any items with damaged packaging are likely to be returned for a full rebate which can be more costly than paying attention to strong materials in the first place.

This means your packaging may have to be a bit stronger than you customarily use. Remember also that the hot, humid summer weather can cause mould and mildew, and your packaging must be able to resist this.

An advertising quirk

In your advertising in Japan, you must never mention a rival or compare your own product with that of the competition. This would be regarded as unacceptable behavior and the belief approaches the strength of a cultural taboo. In addition, hard-sell approaches tend to backfire on both the company and product and should be avoided. Instead you have to inform people about facts and try to persuade them that yours is an excellent product in its own right.

Establishing the right mood and feeling can also be effective. The strong interest in nature, combined with elegance, simplicity and somberness, makes the Japanese particularly responsive to mood and subtle indications of feelings.

English words or phrases on products can also influence, as they carry a feeling of being special and exotic, but take care to ensure that the particular English words chosen are easily pronounceable in Japanese and do not inadvertently mean something rude or downright insulting.

Product promotions may not work as well as you might expect – but things are improving

In the past four decades, giveaways, premiums and special promotions often did not work well as a marketing device. There seemed to be a feeling that in some way the approach was a bit sneaky and an underhand effort to deceive and manipulate an unsuspecting populace. This has begun to change as free or cheaper products began to be sought during the extended recession since 1991.

Worker-Related Issues

Choose carefully the person who will do the hiring

The prevalence of effective networking together with group solidarity means that whoever does the hiring will choose his own kind, such as those who attended his university, come from the same background, or are friends or the friends of friends. It is worth spending time and taking lots of local advice from different sources before you make this first crucial hiring decision. Someone who went to a third rate university can usually be guaranteed not to have access to people who went to a first rate one. Those he hires in turn will also not have the best network access that you need.

It is most important that you make sure this first person is truly mainstream Japanese and not from what was originally a Korean or Chinese family, or from Okinawa. If you do not do this, local prejudices mean that your company could run into difficulties of gaining cooperation further down the track. If you go through a professional recruiting agency, the staff should automatically check this point.

Love those workers!

You must take a strong interest in the problems of your Japanese employees. The relationship with workers is not at all like that in most Western countries, but is a rather feudal situation, where those in charge feel responsibility for those underneath. A person with power in Japan is rather like an old-fashioned strong family head in the West: he is deferred to by the children and others, but in turn they can expect to be protected and cared for properly. It is rather like the situation depicted in the book and film *The Godfather*, where the Mafia in the USA is described as operating in this fashion.

All important Japanese companies offer various perks and subsidies and take care of their workers in a variety of different ways.

As well as the job for life (as you will recall, recently under attack) they offer such things as the provision of housing or else low interest mortgages, subsidized meals, free hot baths, free membership of a sports club (valuable, as sporting facilities are scarce), free tickets to shows and events, free trips and outings, subsidized holidays or even access to a weekend company cottage. Most recipients tend to be permanent employees, graduates, and male. Your company will also be expected to offer perks but not the whole list.

Managers in Japan are widely expected to help sort out problems that are usually regarded as strictly personal in the West. A Japanese manager might be asked for advice about finding a suitable wife for instance, or the company might agree to pay for the funeral of an employee's spouse. It is felt that if workers have problems with money or family, they will not work as well, so it is in the interests of the company to engage in the business of proffering good advice. If you do not do this, either because you find such actions hard to take, or just because you are not Japanese, a worker might feel resentment that the foreign manager does not care enough or understand – and this not only can but will cause long term problems for you. An important and thoroughly reliable employee might even leave your employment for what seems to him a perfectly good a reason even if it seems trivial to you.

If you treat your employees rather like a family member – not too close, perhaps about a cousin in many Western countries – you will not be far out. Setting up a joint venture or running a company in Japan requires the learning of a whole new style of management. It is by no means impossible to do this – many Japanese firms have moved abroad and successfully learned different foreign management styles. It is just as hard for them as it is for you to do things in what is regarded locally to be the proper but very different way.

The pursuit of profit is not the sole goal

A cold-hearted pursuit of profit does not sit easily within the culture and if you stick to your Western practices, you might damage or destroy the human relationships within the company. It is often good to ask yourself what affect a decision might have on the harmony of the group before you make it. Extra profits in the short term that upset people can lead to bigger losses in the long period.

Your staff may choose not to take the holidays they are owed

You will be already be aware that Japanese workers tend to work hard and many are workaholics. It is extremely common for employees not to take their allotted holidays or their sick leave. However, a change appears to be underway, and some of the younger generation have started to question such values and begun to slacken off, at least by more traditional Japanese standards. Most observers expect this trend to continue, and the Japanese gradually to become more like their Western counterparts and indulge in more leisure.

Trade unions are not a problem

Trade unions are enterprise-based and generally are weak. Therefore there is little sense of a working class in opposition to management. When the agricultural workers flocked to the city in the first half of the 20th Century, they brought the attitudes of the village with them. Cooperation, essential for survival in rural Japan, is still the norm. In addition to this, the constant urban labour shortage has meant that people arriving from the countryside could immediately find work, so that there was no hanging around in unemployed groups where they might gain a feeling of working class solidarity with their fellows. In turn, this meant that they were not easily accessible to persuasion by any radical political firebrands.

Loyalty goes to the company one works for, to one's immediate boss, and to a person's work group, not to some vague principle like "working class solidarity". There is no strong identification with "craft" either so that, after suitable training, moving workers from one task to another can be relatively smooth, which has rendered the task of technical innovation easier. It is indeed expected that when times are hard, rather than dismiss workers a company will retrain and move them. Union membership is not high by Western standards and you need expect no particular problems in this area.

Labour turnover is low

Until very recently, workers in large modern companies expected to have a job for life, but things are beginning to change and some large firms are shedding surplus labour. This is not easy to do, as old attitudes die hard. A worker still aims at building up a series of relationships within his or her company and of course anyone who leaves the firm loses this set of relationships. It will never be possible to replace them fully in the new firm which means they will be both less happy and productive workers. Knowing this, workers are keen to stay where they are so labour mobility is low.

Each company also has its own particular spirit, which is first created in early indoctrination programmes and then strengthened in the various group bonding practices, such as daily community singing of the company song, eating and drinking together as a team, socialising after work, or going as a group on company picnics. If a person moves to a different firm, it is difficult to adapt to the particular situation of this new company with its different practices and established relationships, or many at least believe this.

For such reasons, few Japanese willingly contemplate career changes which involve moving to a new company. The common Western habit of building a career by changing jobs and moving sideways and upwards is not part of the culture. In Japan this is done within the company, not by moving outside it. This means that if you observe people starting to leave your company, something may be going seriously wrong and you should consider immediately calling in a local expert to investigate and advise.

One way of increasing the loyalty of your staff is to make sure there are plenty of nice sounding labels and intermediate level posts that your workers can aim for. If you become the sort of company that consists solely of expatriate managers and Japanese workers, the latter will know they have little chance of promotion and consequently feel less loyal.

The annual wage demand

Awareness of the changing seasons and a need for adjusting the pattern of behavior is widespread and this even includes wage negotiations. You can expect to face an annual wage demand session with your company trade union. April is the traditional month for going through the process of negotiation and is the time when industrial disputes may occur in the so-called "Spring Offensive". The public service and private industry tend to go through this annual routine about one month apart. With the falling prices and wages seen during the first years of the new millennium, there is really less reason for this annual round but old habits are hard to break.

Staff cost can be greater than you think

You will probably find that you will have to pay your staff more than a Japanese company would. If you do not do so, you could fail to attract the necessary talent. This is not mere exploitation of you as a foreigner but is the result of several factors all pushing for a need for higher pay. There is the lack of permanent employment you offer compared with a traditional Japanese company, for which the employees will feel he needs compensating. This particular factor is weakening as even the big name players, such as Toshiba, lay off workers these days if times are hard.

The workers will also face practical difficulties when working with foreigners. They will have to speak reasonable English and that is not as common a skill, say, as in Hong Kong or Singapore. Despite more people now studying English, such workers command a premium for their ability. Finally, there is a general feeling of uncertainty when working with non-Japanese and know they will be looked down upon by the employees of proper Japanese firms. A higher financial reward helps to compensate for all this.

Note that virtually everyone is paid in cash in Japan and cheques are an unusual and rather unpopular way of paying wages or salaries. Japan is still pretty much a cash economy and you will find yourself using actual money a lot rather than credit cards. You might even find it difficult to make use of a credit card at all.

Two bonuses a year and other allowances

If running a firm in Japan, you will have to pay your staff a bonus twice a year. The first will occur in early summer around June and the second at the end of the year. Although sizeable, at one to three months salary each time, the bonuses can serve as a strong incentive system, for example you might make the size dependent on the state of the company's profits, share of market, or growth in turnover. Only if times are really hard can the bonus be zero. Pension plans are not common in Japan, and instead you will probably have to pay a severance bonus, which might amount to about two years' salary. In addition, you should expect to pay your staff various allowances, perhaps for commuting, working overtime, as holiday pay, or for housing. Such allowances are common in large Japanese companies, which as you know may also provide things such as a subsidized canteen, access to a holiday cottage, free membership of clubs, or cheap housing.

Keep quiet about costs

If you have a problem with costs, it would be a bad idea to discuss it with ordinary workers or even mention it in front of them. Such matters are seen as purely an affair of management. You can and should discuss the issue carefully with your Japanese managers, soliciting ideas and views, remembering to be careful not to place the blame on any person or department. All problems require a solution and the restoration of harmony rather than finding someone to blame. Remember to be as indirect as possible and the problem will be tackled better by all.

Temper temper!

Never lose your temper or shout. It simply is not the way things are done and it will harm your reputation at once. Rather than see it as a cultural difference between your country and Japan, they are likely to be secretly amused by your childish inability to control your emotions and you will forfeit their respect. In hierarchical Japan it makes life very difficult for all if the boss is despised by those underneath.

If you feel a need to reprimand someone, it is usually better to get one of your Japanese managers to do this, rather than tackle it yourself. He will be able to do it smoothly in an appropriate manner and without upsetting the existing good working relationship.

Your workers will expect you to socialize

This means you will have to set up, or at least attend, various informal drinking sessions after work and you also have to organize parties at the end of the year. Whenever someone leaves you should arrange a party, make a speech, and accept that later in the evening the gathering may turn into something like an amateur talent show at which all are expected to sing individually. This includes you! A poor performance on your part would not raise your status in the eyes of the staff so that it would be wise to practise before the event. As the boss you will be expected to leave relatively early, allowing the underlings to relax and enjoy themselves in your absence. Please don't stay to the bitter end!

You will also be invited to attend various events which in the West would usually be restricted to the private family and a few close friends; these include weddings and funerals. If you try to duck out of such obligations, it would lead to low morale and a reduction in work efficiency.

Orders are the exact opposite of holy

You should try to avoid issuing instructions and orders to your staff in the usual Western way. A simple *request* is quite sufficient in Japan and carries the force of an order. Japanese people are accustomed to picking up hints and they will regard what might seem like a diffident suggestion from the person above as a strong requirement. It is considered unnecessarily harsh and even vindictive to issue a direct order. In the culture, "It would be nice if something were..." is regarded as an order, while "Would you mind going..." is seen as a very strong directive, as in this instance the person has been specifically given an instruction.

Let's walk the line

It is important not to issue a request (i.e. an indirect order) to someone who is not immediately below you in the hierarchy, i.e., it is essential to go down the line of authority. Deviation from this principle is liable to cause havoc, your action will be discussed, and all sorts of hidden motives for it will be sought by the staff. In all probability you intended none of the possibly fiendish motives they are likely to ascribe to you. If you jump line authority, someone somewhere will inevitably be offended by your action and resent it.

If you cause offence to someone, however inadvertently, you make an enemy of them. They may then try to take revenge upon you in some way: as a minimum they might refuse to help when they could, and possibly they may actively work behind the scenes to obstruct you. The superficial mask will conceal their real intentions and you may never discover what's going on. If you are looking for a phrase to describe the best way of running a successful and profitable company in Japan, it would be "Hierarchical Harmony".

No surprises!

Never try to surprise your staff in any way, however gracious or cordial it may seem to you. The habit of giving surprise parties, popular in America, should be avoided at all costs. In Europe they are often seen as a somewhat eccentric thing to do, but most Japanese positively hate them. When you think about it, surprise parties are bound to sit uncomfortably in a formal society that constantly worries about behaving correctly and greatly fears loss of face.

Decisions should emerge after discussions and soundings out, so that everyone is aware of what is in the wind. You can easily get what you want, as the discussions are a formality really. If you suddenly surprise your staff, perhaps doing something nice for them, they will tend to wonder what the cunning foreigners are up to now and will probably waste time worrying about it, seeking your hidden agenda. Since you do not have one, they will search in vain behind the surface for the reality they expect to see.

Public praise of an individual is not a good idea

The socially acceptable view is that the entire group should share in any success, rather than any particular individual getting the credit. If someone really has done well, you could tell them this in the privacy of your office. If you do this, make sure that you do not also say "By the way, while you are here I thought we might do..." because if you do, he or she will think that this was your real motive for inviting them and, understanding they are being reprimanded, will tend not believe a word of the praise you just gave them.

Promoting staff can be a problem

Your instinct will probably be to promote the best and most hardworking members of staff, i.e., those who stand out as possessing obvious ability. If you do this, you can alienate all your staff, perhaps even including those you promoted. Such people are often seen as too individualistic and can be unpopular within their groups. Because a manager must tactfully handle delicate human relationships, this type of person can face serious trouble after being promoted to a managerial position. The ideal candidate for promotion in Japan is often the person who is best at keeping group harmony and achieving what is needed in an indirect fashion. Although promotions on merit are increasing, this is still not the automatic way of doing things. Seniority and the ability to get along with people are still the main determinants in many companies.

People do not expect to get promoted regularly or quickly but look forward to moving up at about the same rate as those in their seniority group. If you set up a new firm you will gain a few years experience of the system before you have to think of promotions anyway. Once promotions begin, the seniority system ensures that your labour costs will start to rise.

Blood groups and you

You should not be surprised if your Japanese staff seem particularly knowledgeable about their colleagues' blood groups. There is heavy symbolism about blood types and it is widely believed that they determine a person's basic character. Blood groups are taken so seriously that they might even be the decider about whether a particular person will be employed or not. Many people put their blood group on their *résumé* for this reason.

A surprisingly high number of well-educated and powerful Japanese subscribe to blood group typing, in much the same way that people often read their newspaper horoscopes in the West.

Table 9.1 Common beliefs about blood group types

Type A	This is the most commonly found group in Japan and is felt to indicate a conservative, shy person, interested in detail and maintaining group harmony i.e., the traditionally desirable type of Japanese. It is felt good for a woman to be in this group, but type A is essentially not leadership material.
Type AB	Type AB is a poor group to be in, as it indicates an unsettled person (probably because it is seen as a mixed rather than a single group), one who is given to highs and lows, and is generally not a good mixer.
Type B	Group B represents individuality, the lone wolf type, and perhaps a bit selfish. Such a person tends to know where he or she is going and how to get there. This type has not been the desirable norm in the past, but might become more so if Japan Westernizes more.
Type O	Type O people are seen as leaders, the kind of people who have a good view of overall strategy and goals; they are group-oriented, but not just an ordinary member of it. This of course is a very desirable type of blood to have: a bank president would represent this group in the minds of many people.

Don't show favors

You need to be particularly careful never to show favors to individual members of staff, especially to young women. They can react badly and you can easily upset the equilibrium of the whole office. Rumors are likely to fly around both the group and the wider company, with the result that work efficiency could fall. Paying due respect for the tight social structure of Japan, you must try to treat everyone equally within the stratum they occupy. If you single out anyone in any way it violently shakes the web of relationships and attracts everybody's attention.

If you are male, you should never invite a young female worker to have lunch or even a cup of coffee with you. She will be embarrassed and may not know what to say, it will immediately generate a lot of office gossip, and it will be widely assumed that you are having an affair. People meet together and go around in groups in Japan, not in couples. People always go for lunch or coffee with their own work group not with an outsider.

When Working for a Japanese Company

If you take a job in a company in Japan, as opposed to running your own firm, there are certain things you can expect to find.

The honorary guest

As a newcomer you will not automatically be accepted as a full member of the group or the company. This would be true, even if you were Japanese – you have to be assimilated into the particular company's attitudes and structure. You start this process by being a quiet, observant member of a team which will gradually come to accept you as a member. You have to serve your time in a sort of apprenticeship to the team.

What the heck am I supposed to do?

You will rarely have a job description or have any one explain to you how to do the job you have been given. Learning in Japan is traditionally done by watching, listening and imitating, rather than by someone delivering a structured outline of a discipline. This applies in business, as well as in areas as diverse as flower arranging and pottery making. Zen Buddhism eschews formal teaching as well as the use of logic, and its influence is powerful.

Sitting around with little to do can be frustrating and you will probably feel much of your time is being wasted or your abilities underused. There is not much that you can do about it and making waves by complaining will not endear you to your boss or group. You are expected to watch, learn as you go, and at the same time listen to and pick up advice, which itself will be low key and perhaps shyly offered. It would be exceptional to be put through a formal training programme. Many Japanese learn the ropes by observation and practical on-the-job experience over a period of years.

What can make it more difficult for you is that it is bad manners to ask direct questions of your superior, so that if you are working in a Japanese company and do not know what you should be doing, your normal response (to ask your boss) is not available. You might try quietly indicating that you have a problem, by starting by explaining that you regrettably know too little about the firm, and of course blaming yourself for this inadequacy, before going on to suggest you would benefit from learning more about your role. This might smack of grovelling to some Westerners but it is acceptable in Japan and it might just work.

One thing to remember is that you cannot be a clock watcher and leave right on the stipulated time. The whole team will probably wait for their boss to leave before they feel that it is alright for them to do so. If you up and go at the stipulated hour, you will certainly be criticized for this within your group.

Up team, up team, up team!

You will normally work and live as a team. This means you will be in an open-plan office with your group, go with them for coffee and lunch breaks, and sometimes accompany them out after work. When at work, you should not try to make friends outside your team, or (worse) leave them in order to sit with another group. If you do such things, then the chances are you will be criticized by your colleagues behind your back, they might well complain to the boss about your unseemly actions, and you could easily be reprimanded for this "misbehavior". In Japan it is always considered wrong to go against the group or try to move outside it in any way.

Within the team

It would not be a good idea to joke or flirt with a member of the opposite sex. He or she would be embarrassed and, far worse, you are breaking the mores of the group by trying to divide it. Casual flirting, joking and teasing are not normal in Japanese culture.

You are also expected to give the team your full support as you strengthen your position within it. If you think things could be done better in some way, *keep quiet and don't make suggestions*. Any proposals by you will result in your acceptance into the team being delayed or even prevented. All suggestions will be taken as veiled criticisms of the team or company and reveal you to be an outsider who is not even trying to meld into the company in proper fashion.

You just might get close enough to the members of your team for them to ask you to use their given names. It is not really likely, but if it happens it means that the previously strict insistence on formality is slackening a little. Remember never to use the given name of your superiors, even if your team colleagues have invited you to use their names, as this would be regarded as *lesé-majesté*.

Last minute invitations

You are likely to receive invitations towards the last minute and might find that you are suddenly invited to a meeting, or to go to a party, almost out of the blue. It would not help you to ask why you were not notified earlier and any effort to make your displeasure felt is likely to irritate your colleagues and superiors and so backfire on you.

Oh those meetings!

Expect you will have to attend many business meetings with your team. It is best to keep quiet in them. No decisions will be made as a result of what people say anyway; the meetings are mostly to rubber stamp what has been decided once private discussions at higher levels have reached a consensus. The facade of democratic participation in the decision making process is preserved and the difference between appearance and reality continues to be accepted. Under no circumstances should you make a suggestion for a new way of doing things, or complain about your position in the company, or the actions (or lack of action) of any particular person. Not only will it do no good, you will become unpopular and make personal enemies.

Chewing on your pen

If you chew on your pen or pencil, or even stick it in your mouth or tap your teeth with it, you will be regarded as a childish, immature individual by those around you who are likely to gossip behind your back about the fact that you probably were not weaned properly.

You're never too ill to work

If you get sick, such as a cold, you will still be expected to go to the office. The work ethic is strong and you are expected to make it in unless you are just about dying. One day off on health grounds is permissible, but rarely do people seem to take more than two. If you stay home for longer than that, you can expect to be criticized when you return to work for being less than dedicated to the company.

Why am I only rich on paper?

Japan is expensive, particularly around the Tokyo area. Your salary which looked great on paper back home will almost certainly prove to be inadequate and you will probably have to budget carefully. If you can get accommodation from the company, grab it, whatever it looks like! Remember that when abroad, living like a local is cheaper than trying to reproduce the styles of your own country. To save money, you may quickly have to adjust your ideas about what constitutes normal eating, entertainment and travel.

You can't be friendly to your superiors

As a non-senior member of the firm you should try to be respectful to everyone above you and in particular try to be formal in your dress, speech, and behavior. They will think more highly of you if you do. If you adopt what to you is a natural friendliness based on your own culture it will count against you. This is true whether you are a temporary exchange student or an executive making a career in Japan.

Your superiors are beyond praise

It's best not to praise your superior for something he did, such as making a particularly impressive speech or a brilliant view he expressed at a meeting. If you do, it will not please him. On the contrary, he will probably be annoyed. In contrast to your culture, praising your boss suggests that by daring to offer a view about his behavior you are putting yourself on a pedestal above him. This really seems quite shocking.

"Do you speak English?"

Total strangers on trains or buses are likely to try to engage you in conversation in order to improve their English. It is fun at first, but eventually can become very tedious. If you speak a little foreign language you could try answering in Swedish or whatever "I don't understand", which gets you off the hook. Of course if they happen to speak Swedish you are in trouble! However few Japanese are good at languages and this would be an unlikely event.

Don't forget you need to learn a few phrases of Japanese to be polite as well as to help you in your job. The more you know, the more people tend to respond positively to you.

Meeting someone on the street

If the Japanese run into someone on the street, whether by accident or prearrangement, they do not shout and wave from a distance but wait until they get very close then nod or bow to each other. If you run into a Japanese friend, they would not appreciate you shouting greetings across the road in friendly fashion. If the person is superior to you in the firm, a bow is polite, but a wave is considered to be rude.

Culture shock

If this is your first time abroad, you can expect to be surprised and sometimes shocked by what you observe. It will help if you follow the advice scattered throughout the book on how to behave. In particular, while at work you must dress and behave formally, avoid jokes, horseplay and casual behavior, and be respectful at all times. If in doubt or an incident arises, it is best to apologize immediately for not understanding what is going on or not doing it properly. If you do not appreciate what has happened or what the problem is, apologize anyway! An apology given immediately accompanied by a small bow gets you out of trouble in most cases.

Try to resist the urge to look down on people who obey rules quite different from your own. Do not voice your criticisms openly, especially to another Japanese person, however Westernized and friendly they may seem. If you must let off steam, do it in private with someone from your country. Culture shock can be powerful and unpleasant at first. Eventually you will come out of it; by then you will probably have learned to respect and admire the people and country of Japan. There is long, rich and fascinating culture here and it is at your fingertips - so grab the opportunity and learn what you can at first hand.

Ten: How to Treat Visitors to Your Country

Early Matters

Few Japanese fly solo

When the Japanese come to visit you in your country, they are likely to send a team. Rarely will a solitary Japanese be sent abroad. The companies prefer to send a team because decision making is a consensus activity and a single person could not usually commit the company to anything. Apart from that, few Japanese really enjoy being abroad on their own, although a change is occurring with some young people starting to travel abroad as individuals and even live adventurously. The people you are likely to be dealing with are usually too conservative and mature to tackle personal adventures in this way.

How can I help you?

It is a good idea to ask them in advance what they wish to discuss and see in your company. This allows you to put a draft agenda together and warn your colleagues that they should think about the issues and be ready for the meetings. Find out also if the Japanese want you to supply an interpreter and if so find a good one, preferably a native speaker. If you are seen to be coping with problems as they arise, rather than planning carefully in advance, the Japanese will be unimpressed with your inability to manage details.

A home from home

A Japanese-owned hotel is a good base for them. It makes their life simpler, as their particular needs will be catered for and they can relax and communicate with the staff. Imagine if you had to stay in a hotel in a foreign country with totally different foods and habits but where the staff did not speak any English at all! They will also not wish to be put in a room numbered 4, 44 or 444, which could happen in a Western hotel and could make them feel uneasy. Organize a car to pick them up at the hotel and return them at the end of the day.

A senior male executive should meet them in at the airport or wherever

Someone male and high in your company possessing an important-sounding title is best. You may have to persuade him to

185

make time in a busy schedule but it will be worth it to your company. Serve them coffee, tea, or orange juice immediately upon arrival. In Japan it is customary to serve drinks without offering a choice, and they are often surprised and sometimes even a bit put out to be offered one. A tour of your premises would be appreciated. Japanese companies are often loath to let foreigners see their research laboratories in case technical or commercial secrets leak out. This means that they will not be surprised or annoyed when being shown round if part of your buildings are "Closed for rewiring and maintenance" or the like.

Take plenty of photographs of them

If your company can run to a male photographer, it is a good idea to have him accompany them and take photographs of their visit. If you can stand the cost, he could cover their time around the city, as well as when they are at your company. A posed group photograph with your CEO or President would be valuable, as would a photograph with one or more of your local civic leaders if this could be arranged. If you mount the photographs in an attractive album (don't forget your company logo!) and present it before they leave, the gift would impress your visitors immensely, become a treasured memento, and should help to cement the business relationship.

Where and How to Meet

The formal conference room is best

It is better not to hold the meetings in your own office at work, unless of course you are the president occupying a magnificent suite, because in Japan this would be considered not formal enough. If for some reason you have to use your own office, rather than an impressive directors' meeting room etc., then it would be a good idea to apologize for the lack of space, and explain politely that this is the way things are done in your country. They are likely to accept this, without feeling upset or demeaned, if you put it politely.

Hey look, our annual report!

If you can get hold of one, place a copy of their company's latest annual report clearly visible on a nearby table. This will make an impression – it shows you have done your homework and are really interested in the company. Likewise, if you can arrange for them to observe an easily identifiable Japanese government report it would improve the atmosphere. They will be aware that this has been done specially for their visit, but they constantly expect a distinction between appearance and reality and will feel good about your actions. A small Japanese flag, along with your own, on the negotiating table would impress them with your forethought too. A Japanese painting or scroll on the wall would go down well and provides a point for the early pre-business small-talk as long as you know enough about it to hold your own (see Table 1.2 Some standard symbolism in the arts, p.7).

Remember the social etiquette about meetings in Japan and observe them as much as is practical. This includes things like seating them facing the door and ensuring there are a couple of nearby empty small rooms, for caucusing by both sides during the meetings.

You need sufficient copies of documents – and some equipment

Each member of their team needs their own copy of all documents. Your meeting room should have complete audiovisual facilities – and ones that are functioning. Your visitors may have brought a video to show without informing you in advance and you would not want to have to make them wait while you sent a gopher to scour the building. Japanese companies routinely take care of such details. Make sure there are any other facilities that might be needed, such as whiteboards and pens, along with an eraser that will work with those pens, and of course notepaper.

A presentation pack

It would be a good idea to put together a presentation pack and give one copy to each member of their group. This could contain all the documents and background information about your company that they might need. It would be worth trying to make it look impressive and remember to include plenty of data and hard information; you can leave out all glossy PR documents that aim to "sell" the company but provide little in the way of facts; these tend to depress Japanese visitors rather than impress them.

Expect to be given gifts

As the visitors, their team will probably arrive with gifts for you. These will probably be small and should be received by your team with due courtesy. Remember to open such gifts later, unless they encourage you to open them there and then. If you took presents with you to Japan on your last visit, you do not have to supply them with more. If you do, it can spark off a whole new round of gift-giving, as they will feel that they now owe you one.

Take note!

If anyone explains anything in Japan, it is common for people to take notes. If your entire team just sits and listens the speaker may well feel insulted and decide that you do not really care for him or his company. You might choose to delegate someone to ostentatiously take notes, even if you do not feel you really need them. You would not wish to risk losing a contract for what might seem such a small matter to you.

Try not to point with your finger

You should be aware that when you show people the way, it is customary in Japan to indicate by pointing with the whole hand, palm uppermost, rather than with a finger. This whole hand gesture might look rather gracious but distinctly old-fashioned in many Western countries, but your visitors will understand and appreciate it. You might notice that if your Japanese visitors do point (rather rare), they tend to extend the middle finger in a gesture that can sometimes look rude in the West, especially in North America.

Accompany them through the door not just stand inside the room

When they leave, go outside with them. You should also wave them off, and wait for them to disappear out of sight, before closing the door. If you are not the main host, and they merely visited your section or department on the way to somewhere else, you should still accompany them a little way, outside the door of your section and as far as the lift door if they are heading there. Pressing the button to summon the lift for them would be a friendly gesture and would be noticed favorably; this would always be done for you in Japan.

Social Aspects

A home visit is not necessary

It is in fact better not to invite a visiting Japanese team or person to your home on their first visit to your country. An invitation home may seem natural and friendly to you but if you invite them on a first visit, the Japanese are likely to wonder about you and might just think that it shows that you are not a serious person. They could even worry that your business intentions are not yet certain and you are running them around a bit. It is usually best to wait for a subsequent visit before inviting them to visit your home.

At one time it did not really matter if you never took a Japanese visitor to your home, but things are changing as they travel abroad more. A Japanese businessman with wide foreign experience is likely to know that it is normal in your society to invite important visitors home, may already have experienced it himself, and might be interested in seeing how you live. If eventually you invite him home for dinner, it will appear as a generous gesture on your part and a mark of sincere respect.

If you invite your guests home, remember not to invite them round to look at the house, even if they comment on how nice and spacious it all is. It would particularly embarrass them to be shown your bedrooms, which are regarded as entirely a matter for the house owner. The normal living area, and of course the toilet, is all they will expect to see.

If you should entertain at home, observe that however informal the occasion, Japanese generally feel very bad about drinking directly from the bottle or the can. Remember always to supply them with a glass, even if all your own friends are standing around the barbecue upending bottles in friendly fashion.

Huge meals are also unJapanese and they might feel unable to cope or even feel slightly sick if given a large slab of meat. It is better to serve something that naturally comes in small pieces and does not need cutting up – remember, they are not keen on eating with their fingers.

Remember to pay back any hospitality you may owe
If you receive visitors from Japan who have already entertained you in that country, you must reciprocate properly. You should make every effort to impress them and do it as well as possible. A meal in a good Japanese restaurant is fine, but it must be of high quality. When looking for a place to take their team for the evening, it is a good idea to avoid any Japanese restaurant which does not have other Japanese eating there regularly. If local Japanese do not go, then it is not good enough for your purposes. The only slight problem with a Japanese restaurant is that your visitors might try to pay the bill. You can politely foil them (see "U-pay – but most discreetly", p.190). A good Chinese restaurant is virtually always acceptable, as most Japanese enjoy Chinese food, but again you must make sure it is a good one. Italian food is usually popular and seafood is always liked. Many sophisticated Japanese, particularly those who travel and do business, now regard

most Western food as normal and enjoy it, so what you feed visitors is of less importance than its need to be of high quality.

Above all, the entertainment venue must be impressive

If you can, you should choose one with a magnificent view or a unique atmosphere. Recall that the Japanese spend huge sums of money on entertaining and you must not appear to be mean – try to really make it a night to remember. That splendid evening out will help future business and give you something to reminisce over the next time you are in Japan. Get your entire team there for the dinner, which the Japanese visitors will see as part of the business negotiations, and do not try to handle it alone. This would be a good opportunity to present them with the souvenirs of their visit – arrange for something which displays your company logo if you can, to act as a permanent reminder.

U-pay – but most discretely

At the end of the meal, expect the Japanese visitors will offer to pay the bill but do not let them. Politeness dictates that they offer, but you are expected to refuse graciously and carry on doing so. It is best to arrange with the restaurant in advance that you will pay the bill later, or that they should send it directly to your company, rather than doing this in front of the visitors. If this is not possible, get one of your underlings to pay unobtrusively and well away from the table; settling up is regarded as a crude activity which should be hidden from guests.

To end the evening

It is customary in Japan to take your guests on to a nightclub etc., after dinner. They would appreciate you doing the same, if the situation in your town permits this. That would be much more acceptable than inviting them home for a drink etc., for this might seem strange and perhaps even a little upsetting or intimidating to them.

A personal folder about your city is a good idea

Each member of their team should get a folder. Again, this could usefully have your company logo on the cover to remind them when they are back in Japan who went to all this effort and is worth dealing with. The information should contain a good map, clearly showing the local restaurants (including all the Japanese ones), respectable bars and nightclubs, and any hotel that is owned by or specializes in catering for Japanese. Brochures for any special tourist sites should also be included and, if one exists, a pamphlet containing a brief history of your town. If one does not exist (check with your local history society) you could write your own, where of course you can mention your company in favourable terms! Such a pamphlet could be considered an investment as it would naturally work well in all your other foreign business dealings.

Social or cultural events

If you know their team might be interested in a particular local event, particularly if their leader is or else they happen to mention any such event, then it is up to you to buy them tickets. This might perhaps be an exhibition or a sporting contest and you should escort them there. Theatre tickets too would be appreciated, especially to a well publicized and hard-to-get-to show, as this demonstrates that you are making a special effort on their behalf.

A Few Other Issues

Why has he climbed in the back of my car?

Do not be surprised if your visiting Japanese gets into the back of your car rather than the front. If it makes you feel like a chauffeur, do not take offence. In Japan, it is customary to get in the back, and not sit next to the driver. Your visitor is simply following normal custom and does not intend to insult you in any way. You can avoid any embarrassment if you wish: as you approach your vehicle together, you could ask them to sit in front with you and say they will get a much better view – your sensitive visitor should take the cue.

Why didn't he open my door?

After you have walked round, unlocked his door and let him in first, it is probable that he will sit there and wait for you to get in. You should not expect your Japanese visitor to lean over and open your driver's door for you. This is often regarded a polite custom in the West, but it is not so in Japan. There the driver is in charge of all doors and locks, and the passenger is regarded as a guest who should never interfere with the things that the host owns.

Why is he asking me all these questions?

Do not be surprised if visiting Japanese take what seems to you an inordinate interest in the way things are done and the way people live in your country. In part this is a matter of an almost obsessional interest in details and a compulsion to learn. However, in some cases it is really a sort of personal marketing survey, conducted by your guests. They are likely to file a report in writing on what they observed and this will go into the company records for possible later use in product development, including minor adjustments that may make one or more of their goods more suitable for export to your market.

Eleven: If you are a Woman

Some Specific Problems of Being Female

Women can expect to suffer certain additional challenges

It is easier for men to operate in Japan, owing to the chauvinist attitude of most Japanese males. It does not mean that only men must be sent to Japan, but it does mean that you will face more frustration and have to work even harder than the men around you. If the ironic question "So what else is new?" just popped into your mind, be prepared for it to be even worse while over there. The fact that you are a woman is more worrying to a Japanese male than you being foreign. Many seemingly sophisticated Japanese do not really know how to treat women in business; they are often afraid of you, and they may well be terrified that they will behave incorrectly and make some kind of mistake. This is particularly so if you are dealing with a smaller company, or one located outside Tokyo, where the people have less experience of foreigners.

If going to Japan, tell them in advance that you are a woman

If you do not do this and they expected a man, when you turn up it can come as a major surprise that can paralyze them for days or longer, adding to your costs and negotiating time.

If you do NOT intend to go to Japan, it's desirable to keep quiet about being a woman!

If you are doing your business by mail and have no plans to visit in person, then they will probably take you more seriously if they do *not* know that you are a woman. Not using your given name and sticking to initials often works well. If you use your first name and they recognize you are female, they are quite likely to address the next letter to your boss, as they will probably assume you are a low level secretary. This is sad but true!

Take extra special care with your business cards

Make sure that you have an impressive and very specific title on your business cards so that they can immediately see that you are high up and have clear responsibilities with power. If you can reasonably include the word "Senior", so much the better. It could be well worth having special cards printed for use in Japan that indicate your precise position and with one or more particularly great sounding titles. Put as many letters after your name as you can justify, perhaps membership of several professional associations or qualifications you have gained in any well-thought-of area. With your card you have to impress them at once in order to show you are both a first-rate human being and possess real power in the company.

Why am I being ignored?

Try not to become annoyed if you are ignored in meetings. If their side asks a question and you reply for your team, it is not uncommon for the Japanese team to ignore what you say and wait for some male colleague to repeat the answer before they will accept it. At the heart is the problem that Japanese males are not used to women having authority, and often seem psychologically incapable of acknowledging the fact that you have real power. You will probably have to work hard to show that you are truly an executive and not merely a lowly gofer. You must stay calm but convey feelings of power and authority if possible.

What to do if someone on their team tries to undermine you

Some Japanese can be incredibly insensitive to Western women and one or two may well try to undermine your authority. Be prepared to face up to the problem and deal with it at once. It is better immediately to (politely) refuse to make tea, do some photocopying or undertake any other mundane task that they suggest you might do. If you do not decline they will believe that you are an office junior or can be treated as such. Remember that they are probably very nervous about how to deal with you and are afraid of making a mistake; ironically, it is often this that encourages them to revert to their accustomed (and somewhat demeaning or clumsily sexually aggressive) way of dealing with women, rather than them deliberately attempting to belittle you. You may have to set the ground rules very early on – not by telling them frankly that you have power but indicating by your attitude and behavior that you possess it. Under no circumstances allow yourself to show emotion which would cheapen you at once.

If you are the team leader, be careful where you sit

It is a good idea to arrange with your colleagues in advance that you will sit in the middle and let them clearly and rather deferentially leave a space for you there then wait for you to sit first. You should never take the seat nearest the door, as in Japan this is the place for really junior people, not powerful executives. As you sit down, if you take a quick look at your team with an instruction for them to be seated it will inform the Japanese that you really *are* the important person there, not something like a note-taker which they might automatically assume. If someone has to undertake a menial task, if you are in charge, make sure that *you* are seen to decide which man will go off and do it – and ask him clearly out loud, using his title if you can, e.g., "Assistant Sales Manager Smith, would you get the copy of the minutes please?".

If you are the leader, say so, and introduce yourself immediately. Should you find that you are being interrupted, it is better to act at once and say politely but firmly that you would prefer to hold all questions until the end. Your aim is to establish your authority fast and then keep firm control.

If you are not the team leader, the Japanese team may ignore you during the introductions. If this occurs, it suggests that they may have seen you as merely an "Office Lady" and again it is desirable that you act. You must get your leader to introduce you *at once* and with a lot of formality, stressing your job title and role in the company. At the same time the members of your team should try to indicate clear respect, for instance they could all be looking at you and not fiddling in their brief cases.

Warn your male colleagues what you intend to do

Before you go to Japan, it would be a good idea to discuss with all the members of your team the typical Japanese attitudes you will probably encounter and decide what you intend to do about them. In this way, they will understand that when you take action to preserve your authority you are maintaining the whole team's dignity, and you are not trying to put them down in front of foreigners. This can also shorten your stay by speeding up the adjustment process. Try to persuade the men on your team to always use your company title as well as your surname, e.g. "Finance Director Jones can answer that..." You should never let them address you by your given name, which the Japanese would immediately understand as emphasizing your junior status.

Pay no attention to the Japanese Office Ladies around you

Never offer to help any of the OLs who will pop in and out doing various tasks – it is important from the start to ensure that you are seen as a person with power. You should never introduce yourself or even smile sympathetically at them: best ignore them entirely! In a hierarchical society you have to demonstrate to those opposite that you occupy a level well above an OL; if you do not do this, you will be treated the way they are.

Some came running

Do not run or walk quickly inside buildings whether in halls, corridors or rooms. Such behavior is heavily associated with OLs, that lowly group of employees. All office workers, especially females, are expected to look busy at all times and as part of this social charade, women will often jog for example when going to the photocopier. You do not wish to project such an image, as it is servile, and underlines your lack of stature and influence.

Body Language and Dress

Your clothes

You need to dress conservatively. It is particularly important not to wear sexy clothing, like low cut blouses, short skirts, or very bright colors. In such apparel you face two disadvantages: you will encourage passes and sexual harassment; and you will lose respect and authority as the opposite side will see you as a flighty OL. Trouser suits are not really acceptable, although you will see some Westerners wearing them. Make sure you take plenty of tights; you will probably find it difficult to buy locally in your size and they weigh very little so take enough. They must be worn however hot and humid the weather (despite your feeling that stockings may be more comfortable), even when socializing and visiting someone's home. Going about in bare legs would seem rather scandalous.

Keep your jewelry to a minimum; each extra item you put on reduces your authority a bit more. It is best not to use perfume, but you are especially advised to avoid a powerful one, as it would suggest you are something of a fluttering flower rather than a woman of authority. If used, perfume should be very discrete. Few Japanese, other than "Fragrant Flowers", use scent, cologne or other synthetic aids. In Japan, perfume is regarded by some as rather vulgar and maybe is being used to mask other body odors that they would rather not think about.

Your face

Try to keep your face expressionless. Strong facial expressions will be taken to mean you are ultra-emotional and lack stability, judgement and power, so it is best to try to look as impassive as possible. If you happen to be a good poker player, you'll probably do well here!

Your makeup should be minimal if you are to impress. The only heavily made up women the men see are people like flighty OLs, geishas, night club hostesses and prostitutes. These all lack power and can be pushed around at will. You need to distance yourself from the automatic male image of being superior to all heavily made up women.

Eye contact is a difficult area for Western women. If you keep your eyes downcast, the Japanese will assume you are a simple OL and will treat you as such – you definitely need to avoid this danger. On the other hand, if you stare in peoples' eyes, it is challenging and rude! Your best bet is to look in the eyes of the person you are addressing, glance away, then after a short while look back again. Do *not* lower your head or eyes when looking away but instead look over the person's shoulder. If you do this on a regular basis, you are behaving like someone with real authority but you will not be directly challenging their manhood too strongly!

Sitting gracefully

If you can manage it, try not to cross your legs when seated. If possible, keep your feet together; if you find this really difficult, you might get away with crossing them at the ankles. Otherwise you are signalling that you are not a sophisticated person. Crossed legs on a man are considered very bad-mannered if done in the presence of a superior - and are regarded as totally unacceptable in a woman.

It's best not to laugh aloud

If a Japanese woman finds something amusing, she politely tries to conceal the fact, either by keeping her face straight or, if that is impossible, covering her mouth with her hand to hide the smile. You might notice someone doing this in your presence, but remember that they are not laughing at you, merely adopting a gesture of good manners.

If you smile in amusement, the Japanese would notice your lack of politeness in not covering your mouth, but if you laugh out loud, especially throwing your head back at the time, many people would be shocked. It looks like extremely tasteless behavior.

Speak low

You should try to keep your voice pitched as low as you comfortably can. In Japan, as in Thailand, a high pitched "little girl" voice is considered desirable for a well brought-up woman, as it emphasizes she is deferential and subservient. Shop assistants and tour guides often adopt it as a mark of respect to the customer. If your voice is naturally high you will tend to be seen as adopting an inferior "female" role. Try to keep your voice in the lower registers at all times and do not let it squeak up suddenly if your are surprised.

If you are obviously pregnant, it is best to stay home

The Japanese have a rather Victorian attitude towards pregnancy, i.e. it is concealed from view and everyone pretends it does not exist; they would be horrified if you arrived to negotiate in a recognizably pregnant condition. It would also reinforce their view of you as a women rather than an executive, and hence reduce your status and authority. Worse, you would be seen as a person who does not even know how to behave properly. Naturally, if you are pregnant but it does not yet show, you should not inform anyone on their side, nor let your team members mention it, for example as an indication of how keen you are to do business that you still came all that way. Your team's prospects would suffer rather than benefit from transmitting this information.

Go for an image of calm, competent and a bit remote

The Japanese are not used to flamboyant and outgoing female business people and leaders; remember the sort of women they associate with heavy makeup! They tend to treat flamboyant women in the only way they know how, i.e. in totally non business-like ways. If you can emulate the movie persona of Alfred Hitchcock's favourite actress, Grace Kelly, you would do fine. This projects a businesslike image in the culture.

Long loose skirts are the safest

When socializing, at some stage you will probably face the problem of having to sit on the floor and get up again later – long loose skirts are the easiest for this. Be aware that it is easy to damage your tights when regularly getting up and down and be grateful that you remembered to bring plenty of spares with you. Bear in mind that typical Japanese clothing sizes are too small for many Westerners and you might not be able to buy ones that fit.

Kevin Bucknall

Drinking and smoking

When ordering drinks, recall that until recently women were expected to drink wine or *sake*, rather than beer or whiskey which, as in many Western countries, were seen as "men's drinks". If you choose not to follow that rule you should take note of what their leader orders as it is a good idea *never* to order any drink stronger than his. If you should order brandy when he is drinking wine he would lose face with at least some of his colleagues and that might cause him to dislike *you*. Unfair isn't it?

Smoking has long been felt to be unfeminine; in traditional companies women are still not allowed to smoke, even at their office desks. You would certainly be better off not smoking, but for a hardened addict this might be too difficult to contemplate. Then again, there are always nicotine patches to carry you through until you get back to the hotel!

Accept all dinner invitations but be wary of the drinking sessions

If invited out to dinner by their team, you must go – but it is not a bad idea to decline any subsequent invitation to go on for drinks afterwards, however pressing they may be. If you accept, and some Western business women do, you will probably end up in a hostess bar, a strip club, or a karaoke club full of drunken males, singing along to sexy video tapes, and as likely as not you will get sexually harassed. The type of woman normally present on such occasions is not going to object to such behavior, and after a few drinks the Japanese males are likely to treat you in their accustomed manner. Karaoke clubs were once safe and respectable places, but recently the videos have become more sexually explicit or downright pornographic. One advantage of not going on for the drinking session is that you will get more sleep and be in far better shape the following morning than some of the males on your team! If you choose to go out drinking after dinner, you will be plied with drinks. When you want to stop drinking, remember not to empty your glass – an empty glass is a direct signal that you want more.

If your host suggests your team visits a bathhouse

As a woman this will raise problems if you accept. This is another instance where it would be better to decline the invitation and let the men go off on their own. Note that in communal baths one soaps and washes outside the bath, sitting on a small stool and using a small bucket or a tap in the wall, before stepping into the communal water.

199

It can be *very* hot! And that tiny hand towel is much too small to hide behind...

Remember that at a party, the sexes tend to group themselves together
Although women are often not invited to dinner parties, if you get to a general party you will observe the women drift into one group and talk together, the men into another where they drink more. It is tricky for you, as you will probably have little interest in the women's discussion (which in your absence would be in Japanese and they may have little English) but you might feel a bit isolated alone with the men, knocking back the booze.

You can expect to face a barrage of intimate personal questions
You might for instance be asked how old you are; the degree of your affection for your children; do they miss you; how can you bear to leave them to travel abroad; why you have no children yet; how tall are you; how much do you weigh; or are you trying to lose weight?

Table 11.1 Some possible responses to personal questions

If comments are made about your age your age	I'm not as young as I once was! I guess I'm older than I look! I'm working too hard on my career to think about it! The years just seem to go by!
If asked how can you bear to leave your children to come to Japan	They are splendid children and support me a lot. They understand the importance of my work. I miss them of course. The family takes good care of them. There is really no problem, we all get along.
If asked why you have no children	My job comes first, later I shall have some. We are not quite ready yet. I am currently building up my career and intend to start a family later. One day I guess!

Remember that it is quite acceptable for you to make a vague, imprecise response that does not really answer the question.

It is considered polite in Japan to put such questions and the people asking probably feel they are behaving nicely, getting along well with you, and are trying hard by going out of their way to show a friendly interest in your welfare. If you ask them in return (assuming the question would be relevant), you are involved in building up the mutual relationship

You and your PA could usefully think of some more responses of your own before you go; it will be good practice as well as widening your choice of things to say.

Accept any small favors that business people suggest

This might be an offer to lend you a company car for a day, or pick you up to take you to a meeting with a client. If you agree it will please them and will also help cement the relationship. Bear in mind, however, that you might be expected to repay even small favors in some business way in the future. You should try to balance the weight of what you "owe", and repay small favors with equally small ones. You will probably find it hard to initiate the process of doing favors but there is no harm in trying.

Seller beware!

If you are in Japan to sell you will find the above statements and advice apply to you but if you are a buyer you should find it easier. As a general rule, when they want something from you they are often prepared to compromise and adjust their behavior to get what they want. Sound familiar?

Japan is safe for women, but...

You are unlikely to be attacked or mugged on the street. However, you are likely to receive some passes and there is a high degree of probability that if you choose to dine alone in street restaurants you will attract predatory males. The hotel eating places are usually fine.

On the other hand, you should be particularly careful when travelling. Trains and subways, incredibly crowded at rush hour, are notorious for apparently respectable males feeling the legs of women they are pressed up against. If you can manage it, get into the "Women and children only" coach.

Many Japanese men really do seem to believe that all Western women are sexually available, and all they have to do is indicate or ask. Sex in Japan has traditionally been viewed as a simple pleasure and has never had the guilt trip attached that nations with a Christian heritage so often suffer. The balance of sexual mores favored the men, but women too could and did take lovers without severe moral censure.

Aware of the problem of some managers not treating visiting female executives properly, some of the larger companies have started to send their managers on training courses. Here they learn things such as it is incorrect to ogle female breasts and butts, grope women in lifts, or ignore the females when shaking hands at an introductory meeting with foreign groups.

One more thing. Remember that you cannot buy contraceptive pills in Japan so, if relevant to you, take sufficient with you to last your stay, including enough to cover any unexpected extension.

Table 11.2 A checklist for women

Are my clothes conservative and business style?
Have I sufficient pairs of tights with lots of spares?
Have I all the medical supplies I might need?
Are my team aware of detailed Japanese attitudes to women and what I will do to maintain my authority?
Given these Japanese attitudes, are the team aware of what they should do?
Am I clear about where to sit and how to behave?
Have I decided whether to go out drinking "with the boys'?
Have I invented my own list of vague responses to personal questions?

If you find the advice in this book interesting and useful you might be interested in a similar book about China entitled *Chinese Business Etiquette and Culture*. For excerpts and information on availability in trade paperback (US $15.95) or e-book (US $7.50) editions, see:

www.bosonbooks.com/boson/nonfiction/china/china.html

Reviews of *Chinese Business Etiquette and Culture*

"Invaluable!! 5 stars. If you ever need to do business in China then don't start anything until you've read this book. It will save you time, money and your sanity! After reading this book we took advice from it and saved a valuable business deal by using some of the knowledge Kevin Bucknall has compiled from his time spent there. This is a seriously good book even if you just want to travel in China as it tells you all you need to know to get the best from your time there." (Shanghai Expat)

"I have no hesitation in recommending this book. It is a must read for anyone planning to do business in China." (Brian N. Cox)

"This is an excellent book for those who want to do business with China, whether buying, selling or investing there. It is full of practical advice and I thought was well worth the money." (Charles Brennan)

"....this is my favorite of the 'culture' books." (Lipser Accountancy Corporation)

"Chinese Business Etiquette and Culture is a most persuasive book on Chinese culture and society I've ever read. Mr. Bucknall is really an expert on China!" (Jiang Fu)

"Kevin Barry Bucknall manages to make the text not only essential but interesting as well..... While the book isn't for everyone, those who want to do business in China may find they cannot succeed without it." (Rebecca Stow)

"The book is nicely written and is capable to appeal to anyone with an interest in China. In particular, the book would be useful to any aspiring businessman... as well as academics seeking to add to the literature on the importance of cross-cultural influences." (Ee Kheng ANG)

Index

A Select Bibliography
(with my views)

Brannen, Christalyn, *Going to Japan on Business: a quick guide to protocol, travel and language*, Berkeley Calif, Stonebridge Press, 1991.

- A useful and simple start and small enough to carry easily.

Christalyn Brannen and Tracey Wilen, *Doing Business with Japanese Men: a Woman's Handbook*, Berkeley, Calif, Stonebridge Press, 1991.

- Although aimed specifically at foreign women, this contains a lot of useful general information about communication and behavior.

De Mente, Boye Lafayette, *How to do business with the Japanese*, NTC Business Books, Lincolnwood, Ill., 2nd edit, 1993.

- A genuine expert, he provides good information on living in Japan, house prices, etc. and special problems with joint ventures; no index.

De Mente, Boye Lafayette, *Japanese Etiquette & Ethics in Business*, 6th edit, NTC Business Books, Lincolnwood, USA, 1994.

- He explains Japanese words well and has a thorough understanding of culture and business – but more explanation than advice; no index.

Hall Edward T. and Mildred Reed, *Hidden Difference*, Anchor-Doubleday, NY 1987.

- Aimed at the American market, this remains a reasonably good introduction.

JETRO (Japanese External Trade Organization), *Doing Business in Japan*, about 1995, Tokyo.

- A simple booklet, rather better than the one below.

JETRO, *Negotiating with the Japanese: a Guide*, Tokyo, 1994.

- A very undemanding booklet which is no more than a starting place.

Jones, Stephanie, *Working for the Japanese: Myth and Realities*, Macmillan, London, 1991.

- She provides useful information, based on a UK survey about working for an overseas Japanese company.

Kataoka, Hiroko C. with Kusumoto, Tetsuya, Japanese *Cultural Encounters & How to Handle Them*, Lincolnwood Ill USA, Passport Books, 1991.

- This book presents you with a situation in Japan and sets a multiple choice test about what is happening and why. It works quite well as a learning device.

Katzenstein, Gary, *Funny Business: an Outsiders Year in Japan*, Prentice Hall, NY, 1989.

- A simple introduction, easily accessible.

Min Byoung-chul and Reagan, Nevitt, *Ugly Japanese, Ugly American*, 1994, BCM Publishers, Seoul, Korea.

- One page per topic, split into two halves: how Japanese irritate Americans and vice versa. A short, simple, and useful fun introduction.

Mizutani, Osamu and Mizutani, Nobuko, *How to be polite in Japanese*, Japan Times, Tokyo, 1987.

- Primarily aimed at those learning the language, there is still much useful information here.

Rice, Jonathan, *Doing Business in Japan*, BBC Books, 1992

- A helpful straightforward book.

Whitehill, Arthur M., *Japanese Management: tradition and transition*, London, Routledge, 1991.

- A somewhat more academic and analytical approach but helps you to understand what is going on.

Zimmerman, Mark A. *Dealing with the Japanese*, Allen & Unwin, Sydney, 1985

- Based on practical experience, he provides good solid advice about dealing with the Japanese.

The Internet is in a constant state of flux and sites come and go rapidly. Currently, a couple of useful URLS are:

www.geocities.com/Tokyo/7210/japanlink.htm

- This is the Japan Ring home page; many other home pages concerned with a variety of issues in Japan can be accessed from here, by circling round the sites.

www.jetro.go.jp/top/index.ht ml

- JETRO maintains a useful web page that is worth keeping an eye on for official information. Click on the button that says "English", top right unless your reading Japanese is top class.

Useful current newsgroups or forums include:

groups.yahoo.com/group/JapanLiving/

- This is "Japan Living", where expats in Japan or people moving there post messages, some of which you might find interesting. You will have to sign up for Yahoo groups to become a member, but that is free. E-mail:

  JapanLiving–subscribe@yahoogroups.com

Executiveplanet.infopop.cc/groupee/forums/a/frm/f/790605721

- This is the Executive Planet forum that covers doing business in Asia, which uses Boye Lafayette de Mente, a well-known expert on Japan.

Finance.groups.yahoo.com/group/SmallBizJapan

- This deals with matters of interest to small businesses trading or investing in Japan. Again, you have to register. E-mail:

  SmallBizJapan-subscribe@yahoogroups.com

CPSIA information can be obtained at www.ICGtesting.com
Printed in the USA
235916LV00002B/62/A

9 781932 482324